MANTRACKING
THE ULTIMATE GUIDE TO TRACKING MAN OR BEAST

**CO-AUTHORED BY
EXPERT TRACKER**

TERRY GRANT
&
NADINE ROBINSON

978-1-4602-1282-0 Paperback
978-1-4602-1283-7 eBook

First Edition

Printed in Canada.

Cover design and photo editing/design by Tiina Keranen
Interior design created by FriesenPress

Photographs © by Nadine Robinson, except as follows:
Penny Sipkes: 190 (far right)
Steve Foster: 48, 150
Guy Kerr: 139
Supplied by SPOT LLC: 152
Terry Grant: 19 (top left), 42 (top), 46, 89 (top left), 170, 174

Contents

Chapter 1:
Getting started

"Why can't I see any deer?" Warren, my stepfather, said, jerking his head from left to right as we drove down the highway.

"Because you aren't looking," I offered. The rest of us had spotted some lone animals and several groups of deer since we set out. It was fall; there weren't a lot of leaves on the trees. There were four of us in the car; my sister Laurie, my mother, her husband Warren, and me.

"I *am* looking," he said. We were west of Turner Valley, outside Calgary, heading towards the mountains to look for some animals.

"Sure, you're looking," I conceded, "but you aren't seeing. There *is* a difference."

Warren snorted and shook his head gently.

"You're looking at the trees, but you need to see between the trees. Look for horizontal lines and stop focusing on all the vertical ones."

"Nope, I don't see a thing." Warren continued to tap the armrest on the passenger-side door impatiently. "I see trees, I see leaves on the ground, I see rocks, but there is no..." Warren stopped talking and tapping. His head was now following something through the front windshield. He swivelled his head backwards to track it through the window as we passed.

With eyes bigger than a deer's caught in headlights, he said, "There was a deer! I saw a deer!" He was both shocked and amazed at the same time, maybe even a bit proud of himself.

"Great," I replied." Now how many were there?"

Some of us can't see the forest for the trees; some of us will only ever see trees. It could be that we're too busy, or we just don't care. Without the right motivation, we don't pay attention to a lot of details around us. Part of seeing is knowing what you might see, and where you might see it. Part of seeing is being open to the unexpected and not trying too hard, otherwise, you'll probably just see what you expect to see. If you're quite sure you won't see anything, you'll probably be right. It's a fine balance between seeing deer in a field (because you always see them there) and not seeing the bear at the edge of the woods, because you were only focused on seeing deer. Part of seeing is understanding human and animal behaviour and their environment, so that you can find clues to their whereabouts. **Tracking** is about finding those clues that can lead to more clues that lead you to your prey or provide you with valuable information about your prey. **Prey** will be used throughout the book to refer to what is being tracked, but prey is also called quarry, game, the hunted, the missing, and **lost souls** (in Search and Rescue). [New terms will be in bold in the text and included in the glossary.]

Tracking is a huge puzzle and you keep getting little pieces here and there, and finally, you hope, you get the big picture. (But I don't do puzzles – after all, why would you take a perfectly good picture and cut it into pieces?)

Getting down to brass tacks, tracking is about training our eyes to see different things, and learning to pay attention to things that we've almost stopped noticing. Let's face it, there is so much going on around us. The world seems to be speeding up and more seems to be coming our way daily. You couldn't possibly notice everything going on around you; it would be exhausting. We've learned to filter out things we think we don't need to notice just to get through the day.

Think about the last time you made a big purchase, like a new truck. Before you started thinking about a new truck, you probably weren't spending a whole lot of time looking at the other vehicles on the highways. Then, once you decided to buy one, you started noticing trucks everywhere, not necessarily a specific brand. You noticed all kinds of features you might want on your new vehicle: short and long boxes, cabs and extended-cabs, and two-door versus four-door models. You also saw ads in the paper and commercials on television for trucks and paid a lot more attention to them.

Once you bought your truck, you started noticing that very same make, model, and colour truck as yours all over the place. A friend of mine swears up and down that he was the first one in his city to have a certain combination of one particular make, model, and colour of truck. While he may have been the first, and he may have even started a trend, it's more likely that they were around, but he just wasn't paying attention to that detail in his busy world, until it mattered to him.

In a nutshell, we filter out what we think is irrelevant to us at the time.

Tracking is the same. Right now, footprints, twigs and cobwebs may not be relevant to you. It's like looking through binoculars that aren't focused. You see the greens and browns of the forest, but everything's all blurry. I hope this book can help you to focus your eyes to see everything more precisely. Once you learn what each puzzle piece of "**sign**" can tell you, you'll notice footprints and vegetation disturbances with interest. You'll begin noticing not only what is there, but what isn't. Indents left from rocks kicked out of place suddenly become much more fascinating, and a broken cobweb may be the missing piece to solve the puzzle. You'll be more clue and track aware. Once you start looking at things, you'll be amazed at how much you can really see.

You don't even have to go far to practice and start tuning your eyes. Your own front or backyard is an easy place to start, and then you can hone your skills in bigger "backyards."

The aim of this book is to teach you the basics of tracking, starting with an introduction of what it is, how it's used, and how I got my start in tracking. My co-author and I will then help guide you in what to look for, how and where to look for it, and how to interpret it once you find it. Next we'll go over the skills you need as a tracker. Then we'll cover different kinds of sign, tracking in different conditions, and methods of tracking. More tips and tricks follow in the psychology of tracking, including tracking people who do want to be found (Search and Rescue) and those who don't (evasion). We'll also look at what makes tracking easier and how tracking animals is different. From there, the responsibility shifts to you and you'll have to take what you've learned in the book and get outside and practice. For kicks along the way, we've also thrown in some stuff about me, and have tried to answer the usual questions people ask.

This book is written for trackers of all levels, to open up the world of tracking to beginners, and to help an experienced tracker hone his or her skills further and/or act as a refresher course. Most of the content is not difficult to grasp. In fact, once you read and try out a lot of these things, you may find yourself thinking, "Wow, that's so obvious...now." Then we'll know the book worked, as you'll have changed the focus of your attention to more of the world around you.

In addition to helping you notice more of what has always been there, we're hoping to pique your interest in getting outside more, and appreciating our open spaces and fresh air. In ranching, in Search and Rescue, and on television, almost all of my tracking has been done in the "wilderness" – but there isn't much of it left that is still "wild." Every time I go out in the bush, I'm reminded how much we need these spaces. Learn what you're stomping on, and learn to appreciate the forests and fields – not just the cities' cement and steel.

In being outdoors and learning about "sign," we can also learn to minimize our own sign, especially remembering to pack out what we pack in, so that those who follow can enjoy the area as much as we have.

Tracking doesn't have to become a lost art. It's not so mysterious. For thousands of years, people all over the world have been using tracking skills to find food, water, and people and to avoid being killed. You can learn them too.

Bottom line: you can't track down lost cows if you're following moose tracks. You can't see the forest if you're only looking at the trees. Reading this book can't give you every detail about tracking, but it will challenge you to see more and ask better questions towards finding what you're looking for.

Read on, and I'll do my best to pass on some of what I have learned in the past 40 years, through stories and examples, to help keep the art of tracking alive.

Chapter 2:
Uses of tracking

"One thorn of experience is worth a whole wilderness of warning."

James Russell Lowell

"Tracking" stirs up all kinds of pictures in our minds. I've asked a lot of people what they think of when they hear the word "tracking": while some people go prehistoric, others think CSI.

Some people jump way back to cavemen hunting dinosaurs. (Now listen, I'm a cowboy, but I didn't just fall off the turnip truck – we all know that "cavemen" weren't alive when dinosaurs roamed the earth, but plenty of television shows have put all kinds of baloney in our heads). Other, more historically accurate people think of Australian outback-type aboriginal hunters, tracking their dinner or threats to their tribe.

Fast-forward a bit in history (and change continents), and African safaris spring to mind for some people. They imagine a local hunting guide, on foot leading a group of men with big guns and safari gear sitting on elephants, searching out big game or "quarry" so that some rich guy can hang safari trophies on his wall when he gets home.

Tracking also stirs images of camouflaged military men creeping through the jungles of Asia, looking for signs of enemy forces.

Back in North America, Western movies have painted us legendary images of trailers and scouts during cattle drives or on the infamous settlement path out west. In many a John Wayne movie, an Indian scout jumps off his horse (with no saddle), glances at the ground and runs some earth through his fingers. He then confidently pronounces how many people were there, how long they stayed, when they left and in what direction they travelled.

Yeah, tracking has been used for as long as man has been able to put two and two together, and there are plenty of uses for tracking today, though not many people focus on the art.

Turn on the nightly news and you'll see images of modern tracking used in policing and Search and Rescue: police roping off a crime scene to preserve footprint evidence, or dogs sniffing out drugs at the airport, or Search and Rescue teams combing fields for a lost child. Occasionally, we even hear of fugitives being tracked by the law or of illegal border crossings being foiled by trackers.

Tracking takes practice, so modern-day hunters are typically more experienced in tracking than the common Joe. They track prey each season; before and after they shoot it. A lot of people assume that when you shoot an animal, it just drops right there in its tracks, but that doesn't happen much. Hunters will often give a beast time to die peacefully; then they track it to bring home the meat, fur, and/or rack. Of course, if they wound the animal badly, but not mortally, they should also be tracking the prey to complete the harvest properly.

Cowboys on the ranches still operating today use tracking all the time. Whether tracking lost cows that went out grazing and went a little too far, or seeing what predators have been lurking around the chicken coop or barn at night making the animals go wild, tracking is part of the job of a good farmer or cowboy. This is how I cut my teeth in tracking, and got hooked on it.

These conjured images of tracking point to just a few different kinds of tracking. We've mentioned cattle ranchers tracking lost cows, hunters tracking their prey before and after the shot, Search and Rescue teams tracking lost people, the military tracking enemy threats, and police tracking fugitives. Add to this all the people who take their recreational activities, like paintball, or capture the flag, real serious and use tracking to locate opposing team members.

Tracking is also used in science and nature conservation, from entomologists (bug scientists) looking for dung beetles in elephant **feces** to biologists and conservationists looking at beaver dams in marshy areas; from Girl Guide and Scout troops on a nature walk looking for tracks to gamekeepers trying to stop poachers.

In an urban setting, if you've ever had your garbage can knocked over and the garbage spilled everywhere, you may have tried out tracking to see if it was a dog, racoon, bird, or cat that made you do all that cleanup work. Or maybe you were looking for prints outside your window to see if a tomcat was back in the neighbourhood driving your pet housecat to distraction.

Back in the bush, tracking can help you stay safe and prevent you from getting lost. For example, if it's late summer and you happen to be in a berry patch without a lot of berries on the plants, and you notice bear scratches on trees and fresh scat, paying attention can help you realize that you might not be in the best spot just now. Even if you packed bear spray, you'd best be on your way.

Tracking can also be done just for fun. Learning to identify animal tracks, or guessing how many people are up ahead on a trail (and if they're women or men, adults or children), just by their tracks, is a fine way to pass an afternoon. I was pretty honoured the first time I heard someone tell me that the kids at their school don't play hide and seek anymore, they play "Mantracker."

In the end, tracking is still very much alive and well and useful to a lot of people in their jobs, like to cowboys and ranchers, Search and Rescue, the military, and police. Surveyors, loggers, and naturalists could also use a healthy dose of tracking knowledge to stay safe, not to mention all those involved in outdoor recreational pursuits like hunters, hikers, bikers, picnickers, or berry-pickers. My co-author Nadine Robinson and I don't want tracking to become a lost art. And we want to see more people off their couches and in the outdoors. That's why we've written this book.

Tracking can't survive if people don't start paying more attention to what is going on around them. By reading these pages, you'll learn what to pay attention to. Then you can start applying it to different areas of your life – from finding where your dog ran off to, to being more aware of your surroundings so that you don't get lost. While we'd love to have a hand in helping to train the next generation of Search and Rescue volunteers with this book, what would be even better is if we could teach everyone else how not to get lost in the first place!

Do I ever get lost? Yeah, it does happen, but not often in the woods. I feel lost driving in downtown Calgary with all those one-way streets going the opposite direction to where I want to go. A GPS might help me navigate my way around Toronto, but it's not so helpful in tracking. Sure a GPS can tell you where *you* are, but the GPS doesn't know where your prey is. There's no technology or "app" you can use to find your prey; there are no shortcuts. No one is born a tracker: you have to learn to track then practice to get good.

Chapter 3:
How I got here

"You can take the boy out of the country, but you can't take the country out of the boy."

North American Proverb

"Always be kinder than you have to be, but don't take any guff from anybody!"

Old Cowboy saying

I was born in 1957 in Creemore, Ontario. Like every other Canadian boy back then, I played cowboys and Indians and hide-and-seek in the summer and hockey in the winter. I had chores to do and I couldn't go play until they were done. One of my main chores was splitting and carrying in wood.

I was more into the outdoors than some kids. On the weekends, I'd go back into the forest and cut down bush and build stuff. My cousin Dewy and I would make wickiups (small huts) and lean-tos and go back every weekend to play, and to see what the weather and squirrels had done to them. We did a lot of fishing and swimming, and I eventually got a part-time job haying in the summer. Dewy and I would play around on his parent's ranch, and we'd try roping the neighbours' cows (you don't want to rope your own, or they get pretty skittish around you).

I was a Boy Scout for a while, and took away the important motto of "Be Prepared."

Having three sisters primed me for patience, but I knew I'd mastered it when my stepfather, Warren, had me help him tear down houses he'd bought along Wasaga Beach. We tore them down board by board to build us a house. We even ripped down a twelve-room motel. It was a major undertaking. Once I knew how to tear down a house board by board, building one was a piece of cake. Those days started me in my carpentry career and gave me an appreciation for hard work and perseverance.

As soon as I got my driver's licence I headed west to find work on ranches (so did Dewy). Once in Alberta, I pretty much stayed, though I came back to Ontario for a couple of years at one point.

I had my share of non-tracking jobs, too: I did construction, worked in a feed mill, was an apprentice welder, and did shipping and receiving in a welding shop. I also did water well servicing and worked in a rubber factory making radiator hoses. Now I focus on crafting custom furniture and doing renovations.

As a cowboy, I had to learn to track on my own. I got to know the difference between a cow track and a moose track pretty quick. There's no point tracking the wrong one for the better part of an afternoon. I'd be gathering cattle in rough country, looking for fresh cow tracks and any fresh tracks of relevance. I didn't follow the moose tracks anymore once I figured them out, and stayed focused on bringing in the cows.

Even if my cowboy mentors didn't teach me to track, they did teach me about cows and their behaviour. It's pretty tough to track something if you don't understand it.

I also learned what a bear track looked like, and began paying attention to tracks to see if there were cubs or not. And I started aging tracks, so that I knew if I had to change directions in a hurry. You don't want to meet a momma bear ready to defend her cub, unexpected. If you're in a valley and find no tracks, then ten minutes later, on your way out, you see big bear tracks on top of yours, that's when you really want to pay attention, especially if you're on foot.

Then I started walking through different terrains to see what tracks I'd made. If I saw a track already there that I didn't understand, I'd try to make that same track. I'd pivot fast, move quicker or slower, or drag my heel; trying all kinds of stuff until I knew what movements caused what patterns. That's when I started to learn that even if I couldn't see my prey, I could see a lot in their tracks; like hesitation, panic, and exhaustion.

Sometimes I'd find myself turned around in the bush, but was always able to find my way out. Other times, me and the guys, we'd tour around and spend half the day "lost," especially if it was in the city. I'm not good in the city, because everything is the same, with square corners, one-way streets, construction, and stuff like that. I'm just more comfortable in the bush.

My horse also helped me hone my powers of observation. I'd be out looking for cows and my horse would stop and look off in a direction. He'd take a few more steps and stop and look again. The horse had heard or seen something that I hadn't. I started paying more attention when the horse would stop. Sometimes it would take me a few minutes to see what my horse had seen a ways back. Only a damn fool ignores his horse.

Ranching was neat. There was always something new happening, like the time I was called in to work on a movie set. It was called Heaven and Earth, a Japanese production, with more horses under saddle than any movie ever made. It was never shown in Canada, except the premiere, which they invited all the foot soldiers and horse captains to attend (I was a horse captain, of course). That was my first time on the big screen.

As a cowboy, rancher, and hunter, I used my animal tracking skills for nearly 30 years. Then I was trained in mantracking, as a Search and Rescue volunteer, to track lost or injured people in the foothills of the Rockies. I did that on an as-needed basis for 13 years, until the television show really jammed up my schedule. It was 40 years of hard work and a lucky break that landed me on television. The producer of the Mantracker series approached my cousin Dewy at the Toronto Sportsmen's Show.

Dewy and me hanging out at Anchor D

Dewy waiting to rope a calf

Dewy runs the Anchor D Ranch, an outfitting company for tourists and adventurists who want to live like cowboys in Alberta. Dewy was probably the only guy there in a cowboy hat, and they asked him about doing the project. He was not only too busy, but he also didn't know how to track people. So he told them about me.

The producer called on a Tuesday. They came out on the Saturday and shot some video of me on my horse, did some interviews, had dinner, and said, "We'll be in touch." I thought, "Yeah, right, I won't be holding my breath," and I went out to my shop to finish up a coffee table for a client. The following Tuesday, the telephone rang and they said, "You're it, we start filming in May." And that was that.

In each of the 59 episodes we filmed, I used my mantracking skills to track down a team of two people (the prey) in rugged terrain somewhere in North America. They got a head start, and a map. Their goal was to make it to the finish line some 30 kms away before I caught them or before time ran out (they only got 36 hours).

I didn't get a map, but I did get a horse, and a local guide to help me navigate the area. We'd usually run across the prey several times over the two days, but a capture wasn't always possible because of the terrain.

I tracked professional and Olympic athletes, police officers, U.S. marines, opera singers, stay-at-home moms, and everything in between. I even faced off against Shane Doan of the NHL's Phoenix Coyotes and a couple of guitar-pickers from The Road Hammers (a country music band).

Over the six years, I tracked 118 folks and after six seasons on the Mantracker series, I was sad to say goodbye to the show. I'd be lying if I said I don't miss the adrenaline of the chase. When I went out and found people who really didn't want to be found – that was really cool.

So now I'm a part-time cowboy, a part-time carpenter, and a kind of celebrity (or so they keep telling me). I'm always working on some projects of my own, like this book, and some tracking educational material.

When I look back to how it all started, I can't help but think that I just grew up playing outside and it stuck.

Chapter 4:
Tracking and sign awareness

"The education of attention would be an education par excellence."

William James

We've talked about kinds of tracking, and also told you a bit about how I learned to track, but I never really said what tracking is or isn't.

I'm not big on definitions, but to me, **tracking** is the art of identifying and interpreting "sign" to find your prey, or determine relevant information about it/them. Even if you don't find your prey standing at the end of its tracks, tracking can help you figure out the direction they went, when they went, how quickly they were moving, and whether or not they're hurt. Tracking is also known as **sign-cutting** in Search and Rescue, so not surprisingly, tracking begins with awareness of "sign." **Sign** is anything left, moved, taken, or changed by a person or animal as they pass through an area. Also called **spoor**, sign is everything that can point you towards your prey. Sign can be on the ground (**ground sign**), like a footprint, paw print, or hoof print, often called **tracks**. Ground sign can also be much more obvious, like things the prey dropped (cigarette butts, gum wrappers, etc.), or expelled (spit, urine, and feces, for instance). For excretions, I don't have any reason for differentiating them this way, but when I hear **scat**, I think of animal feces, and when I hear **excrement**, I think of human feces, so that's how I'll use those words in the book. Sign can also be **top sign** (sign above the ground) including sign at knee or waist level, like tall grasses bent from a passing traveller, or higher up, like a cobweb broken at chest level, or a tuft of hair or fur caught on a branch.

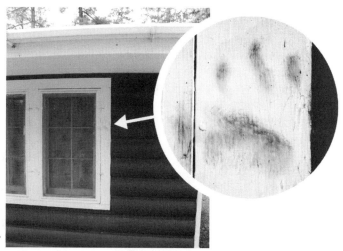

Tracks can also be top sign – like when a bear is curious about what's in a cabin and is peeking in the window.

Sign can be categorized by where it is found (top or ground sign), but I like to think of sign more in terms of what is left, moved, taken, or changed by the prey.

Challenge yourself: Make a list of things that could be taken, changed, or left by prey in a nature setting. Now try and categorize them into groups to explain what has occurred and what you're seeing.

The groupings I think of are:

- *impressions (tracks, body impressions on the ground)*
- *transfers (mud to rock, sand to asphalt, water to dirt)*
- *damage (nibbled branches, bruised vegetation, broken cobwebs, scratches in bark, charred earth)*
- *disturbances (indentations from rocks or branches kicked out of place, paths made in the grass, earth or rocks disturbed from someone climbing, slipping, or falling)*
- *things left behind (fur, fabric, scat, garbage).*

Another way to think of sign is to call it "evidence."

Think of a crime scene. A police officer is sent to a house where a lot of expensive jewellery was stolen. There is a shattered vase on the floor, and a bit of water. The window is open. He finds a trail of footprints on the ground outside the window leading to the front of the house. The officer also notices that the husband looks flushed and is wearing street clothes while his wife is still in her pyjamas. The sign the police officer sees helps him to age the scene (from the amount of water that hasn't evaporated off the floor); the footprints give the officer some physical characteristics of the suspect (shoe size and tread pattern). The trail of prints across the yard shows the direction of travel. Putting this sign together, his next move may be to check the tread pattern on the shoes in the front hall, while looking for fresh mud on them, too.

Just like in a crime scene, nature has all kinds of sign, and if you're looking, it can appear glaringly in or out of place. Sign can show you where your prey slept, cooked, and went afterwards. Their tracks give you a direction to follow. When you can't find tracks, you might find damaged or disturbed vegetation, a piece of thread on a branch, or water transfer onto an otherwise dry rock to stay on their trail. In a sandy area, where there are no tracks, only lines, the lack of sign might point to someone trying to hide their tracks by brushing them away or dragging a leafy branch behind them.

Studying sign gives you all kinds of clues to figure out what the prey is thinking, what they have done, where they're going, what physical condition they're in, how fast they were travelling, how long they stayed in an area, and when they may have left. Becoming **sign-aware** or developing **sign awareness**, then, is knowing *where* to look, and *what* to look for. That makes the next order of business *how* to look for sign.

Chapter 5:
How to look and see

"The question is not what you look at, but what you see."

Henry David Thoreau

"What we see depends mainly on what we look for."

John Lubbock

I've told you to look for ground sign and top sign, with categories of visual sign to look for: impressions, transfers, damage, disturbances, and things left behind. So, you're looking for what is moved, changed, or left by prey. What I haven't done is spend much time explaining how to do that. It would be great if it were as easy as saying "just look," but as my stepdad Warren found out, it's not that easy to find deer just by looking. The good news is that you can be trained to "see."

I use different techniques when I'm looking up close at one track, or trying to find the next sign in the mid-range, or scanning a large area for movement. In each case, part of looking and seeing is remembering to change perspectives, and avoiding going in with too many preconceptions.

Looking up close

Get low to the track (but don't step on evidence of any tracks!) and look at it from different angles. Stand. Kneel. If you need a flatter angle, move back (you don't need to lie down in the muck). Not only does the angle of your line of sight affect your ability to see tracks, but so does the angle of the sun. You want to keep the sun in front of you to give more contrast to the tracks. If you're tracking someone with the sun behind you, you often have to look backwards to see the tracks. Again, without disturbing tracks and sign, move backwards or forwards to see tracks more clearly.

Good lighting makes tracking easier. Long shadows help make tracks stand out. You get long shadows early or late in the day. The sun at high noon often leaves no shadows, so if you think you have a track and are trying to figure out if it is the right one, cover the track with your hat and use a mirror to shine the sun on it from a lower angle to cast shadows, artificially making more contrast as though the sun was lower. Another way to create your own shadows is to use a flashlight or headlamps strapped onto your shins.

Remember there are no straight lines in nature when it comes to tracks. I key in on patterns of straight lines in the terrain. I tracked one girl for two days based on the three parallel lines on the back of her heel print. A track is conclusively human if it has a pattern of straight lines like that.

Keep in mind that some tracks are easier to see further away than up close and vice versa. A deep moose track is clear up close, but take a dozen steps back and it disappears from sight. **Shine**, the silvery imprint from walking in moccasins/or light tread running shoes down a dirt road, is not apparent up close but can be seen at an angle from a distance.

This means that you can actually be too close to a track or at the wrong angle to see it.

Examples of shine on two different roads

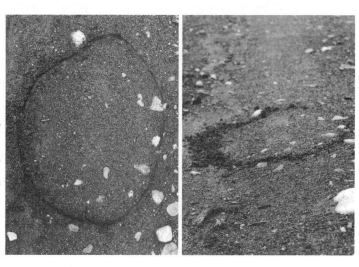

Looking closer at the shine that I'm pointing to in the photo above, I've circled it here and looking straight down, the track isn't visible (left). Backing up and looking at an angle, the shine 'pops' again (right).

I always get asked about shine, and to the best of my knowledge, on a gravel or sand road the weight of the foot makes a shiny area, as it smoothes the ground out as it's pressed down slightly. Moccasins will leave the most shine, but no footprint, whereas Vibram-soled work boots leaves the least shine but the most disturbance because the toe kick will be huge and any foot movement causes much more earth to be disturbed.

How to find the next sign

When looking for the next track or sign, I look at the closest areas first and work my way out in an arc. If you know the average step or stride length of your prey, you can look within that imaginary arc for the next track. You're looking for top and ground sign, and although most will be on the ground, remember to scan at knee height and shoulder height, too.

It's funny, but I've seen hunters so focused on the ground that they miss the plain fact that their quarry is within their sight line. They forget to look up and around.

A tracking stick can help you follow your specific prey. A **tracking stick** can be any kind of stick or pole that is not cumbersome to carry, like an old ski pole, hiking stick, cane, or stick you find in the forest. What makes it a tracking stick is that you mark the width and length of the track and the length of the step on it, with coloured elastics, to help you to narrow your search for sign or identify sign.

Put the tip of the stick at the heel of one track and then put an elastic on the tracking stick, back from its tip at the heel of track behind it to mark the **step length**.

Then put an elastic on the stick to mark the **track width** (across the ball of the foot of the track).

A third elastic marks the **track length;** from the tip of the toe to the end of the heel print.

Using elastics, you don't even need a measuring tape, but if you don't have elastics you could make marks with a knife or a permanent marker. If you can't find a tracking stick, you could grab a broom handle like I did for these photos. If you're in the bush and you forget your stick, it's usually pretty easy to find a piece of deadfall to use as a tracking stick. As a last resort you can compare the track measurements to your own footwear, or measure against your forearm.

When you have your stick marked, you can use it to help you find the next sign. Take your tracking stick, hold it at the end of the last track heel and hold it an inch or so above the ground. Then move the stick in an arc: the tip of the stick should point to where the next track should be, somewhere along that arc. Aside from guiding you to where the next track or sign may be located, the tracking stick also focuses your eyes down to the point of the stick, highlighting about a 12-inch circle, making it easier for you to find the next track or sign.

If you're a golfer, and you've ended up in the rough, you've already done this. You use your golf club to rustle the grass to part it and find your ball by focussing your vision – though some people may think you're just rustling the grass to scare away snakes, which isn't such a bad thing either: I hate snakes.

You won't catch me tracking snakes. They just scare the crap out of me – coming out of nowhere – and BAM they're there, slinking and slithering, flicking their little tongues...they're just sneaky little buggers. (I can't help but think that corporate "snakes" are rightly named, because like their squirmy namesakes, their handshake means nothing, they wriggle out of any situation).

Thanks to my Granny, I grew up not liking anything without shoulders. My Granny was right scared of snakes but she wouldn't think twice about chasing them, like they had trespassed in her garden and so were going to get the what for. She was fun to watch. If she saw one going across the lawn, she'd grab a hoe and then you'd see the soil fly. She cultivated a lot of ground that way. Lucky for the snakes, she'd hit where the snake had been, not where it was then (though she might get an inch off its tail). Unfortunately for her, the hoe might have helped her focus her eyes to the right area, but she didn't factor in the movement of the snake, which isn't a problem when you're looking for tracks or sign.

But let's get back to tracking and how to look when things aren't close up.

Looking mid-range

In the mid-range, you're not looking for the detail in a track, you're looking for a trail of tracks or sign to follow, like shine on a road or silver paths through a field.

Whether tracking on a horse or not, I look for the furthest sign I can see. If it connects back to the track I'm following, I can move faster. Up on a horse, you can track from farther away, because you can see disturbances in the ground farther ahead.

The mid-range is where it's most important to hold your concentration. I remember tracking on a gravel road where I could see little toe kicks; but a noise distracted me and I turned. Unfortunately, when I turned back to the toe kicks, they were "gone." I couldn't find them again, so I had to go back to the last known track and repeat that part of the road, wasting more time than I would have liked.

To find a series of tracks, I use a technique similar to what I'd do in the close-range. I use arc vision, looking at one pie slice of the area at a time to determine possible paths, and eliminate dead ends where there are no tracks. If the prey has used a deceptive tactic, you may not have to follow tracks if you can see far enough ahead to see that the tracks loop back. Then you just stay the course, and more importantly, you don't have to get off your horse.

When I find a track, I look for a **trail,** or a series of tracks or sign from the prey. If I find a conclusive trail, I see how far I can find it in the distance and choose a landmark like a tree near it so that I can keep my focus on that last track and hope to see the trail continue from there. Even with a landmark chosen, however, you may lose the track when you get up to where it was, so you may have to back up a bit until you find it again. There are times when from where I am to 25 feet up ahead, I can see shine, so I can follow every silvery track at a lope on my horse.

If you don't see a trail of tracks, then you have to focus on each track individually. When you're pretty much out of luck, or as I like to say "hooped" and can't see any tracks, for example along a road or path, you check the sides to make sure that your prey didn't jump off in another direction.

A final reminder, even though we're still talking about visual tracking: don't forget to use your other senses as well. Your prey may be hiding in the bushes right beside you and might make a noise that you may miss or choose to ignore if you think you're still on their track. Bottom line, keep looking for conclusive sign, to verify that you're on the right path.

Before moving on to long-range tracking, there is one more mid-long range technique I'd like to throw your way.

Reading what's "on" your eyes

This technique is a bit trickier to explain. You may have experienced something similar when you look at a bright light or television set in a dark room, and then turn it off (or close your eyes). The image you last saw is there "on your eyes" to read: like when someone takes a flash photo of you. You look away but still "see" the light burned on your eyeball.

By way of example, on one road trip once, two of us cowboys were killing time (driving across the Prairies is great the first time but then gets a bit dull). We started trying to read the licence plates of oncoming cars. Our truck was travelling at highway speed and so were the vehicles coming towards us, so there wasn't a lot of time to read the plate – it was really just a quick flash. My bud would try to read the plate like he'd read a book, starting at the left and trying to read each letter individually. He couldn't get past four letters or numbers on the plate. Me, I'd look at the centre of the plate and then look away. Then I could read what was in front of or "on" my eyes. I had no problem remembering most of the plates.

Some plates are easier to remember than others.

With practice, you can do this in conditions with less contrast, until you're ready to use it in a tracking situation. When I'm trying to find a deer my eyes are constantly scanning around me. I look to a new area and then I see a deer "on" my eyes. It isn't really there: I've looked away before my brain can tell me there was a deer back there, so it is probably in the last place I looked. My eyeballs carried the image forward with me, so I look back and there's the deer.

It's like when you do a double take. You're walking down the street, not looking at anything or anyone in particular, and your brain tells you to take a second look at something again, without you really thinking about it. It's because the image of a sweet 1967 Corvette or a fine looking individual was left on your eyes as you kept walking, and your brain doesn't want you to miss out.

Tracking in the distance

If you've completely lost your prey, or you don't have a particular animal you're tracking, but just want to see a deer, for example, you can scan a large area first by looking at the horizon. If your prey has **sky-lined** themselves, they have put themselves between you and the sky; like when they're walking along the crest of a hill, or a ridge. **Sky-lining** is good for trackers and bad for prey because it's always easier to see movement against a backdrop of sky than against the forest floor.

In long-range prey detection, I also use my wide peripheral vision to detect movement and then zone in on it. After checking the horizon, I look for movement, for horizontal lines, for animals at the edge of the forest. I also look for eyeballs. They're round and shiny – and they don't fit with the rest of the bush. Eyeballs also reflect light in darker conditions, so sometimes a flashlight is a great tool for spotting your quarry in low light conditions.

Changing perspectives

Changing perspectives is really important when you're visually tracking. You can't be too focused on one spot or you might miss the forest for the trees. When you're tracking, you have to be looking down, up, side to side, and behind you. You don't know where the sign will be. If you're focused only on ground sign, you might miss important sign left higher up.

Whether it's lace underwear hanging on a branch or a gun range warning sign, it's probably in your best interests to look up.

Some tracks on the ground can't be seen from certain angles, so you'll need to change your perspective by getting lower, higher, closer, farther, up shadow, or downshadow from where you are to get a better bead on sign.

Another way to change perspective is to change your focus. When you sit at a computer all day, you're focused at close range. Any good eye doc will tell you to give your eyes a rest and suggest that you focus on something out the window in the distance every so often. Tracking isn't so different. Sometimes you focus on things close at hand, other times you have to widen your focus.

Back to nature, when tracking animals, you have to change your focus from seeing all of the vertical trees, to seeing horizontal lines – the lines of an animal's back. The trick is that you block out the vertical lines (trees). Look through the trees, not at them. Remember those Magic Eye pictures back in the 1990's where a 'hidden' three-dimensional image would pop out of the two-dimensional puzzle at you, but only if you stopped focusing on the lines and looked past them? You don't focus on it, you focus around it. That's how I blur my eyes to try and "lose the trees."

A hunter I know explains it as looking beside what you want to see, and squinting a touch, and then your peripheral vision will pick up movement in your intended area of focus. Otherwise you find yourself focused on the tree right in front of you and not what may be behind it. You focus on the whole 180 degrees in front of you, while looking straight ahead, without focussing on any one point. The expression "You can't see the forest for the trees" is a good one. If you expect to see trees, then that's what you'll see, and often all you'll see, even though there is so much more there to see.

Changing perspectives is important when you think you've lost the trail. You go back to the last known track and try to look at things from another angle. One of the most forgotten angles is up.

Looking up

While following the trail, don't forget to look up and around. Looking up is something a lot of trackers fail to do because there's usually no reason to look up. There are, however, a number of good reasons to look up: for one, it gives your eyes a break. Just as importantly, there may be unexpected sign hiding in plain sight.

In Search and Rescue (SAR), you're searching more than tracking. A lost child might be hiding up a tree (afraid their parents will be mad at them), or a lost person might climb a tree to try and find the way out or a landmark that they recognize. If you're doing evidence recovery, you might find a bag that someone had flung up into a tree. Unfortunately, if tracking someone with suicidal tendencies, you need to spend more time looking up. Similarly, someone, or part of their clothing, might have got hung up in a tree if they fell from a height, like off a cliff. In SAR, the "searcher cube" that we're taught can be summarized as: look up, look down and all around.

There was a search practice course in Calgary one weekend that I missed out on, but ending up learning from all the same. It seems hard to believe, but while out on training, one of the searchers found the remains of a missing person, hanging in a tree not far off the trail. The people who set up the course didn't look up. The others on the course didn't look up. Probably hundreds of people who walked that trail didn't look up and see the missing person. Obviously, the training day was cancelled, but we all learned a valuable lesson, even those of us not there that day: look up!

Another time, I was doing a short tracking course for SAR where the longest bearing was 20 yards. I'd set it up as a race to see who could find the most sign (cigarette butts, pop cans, etc.) while looking for flags to signal waypoints and the finish of the race. The course was designed to force you to look up and behind you. If you didn't, you wouldn't be able to complete the course. That's what happened to one team of three guys. They were good: they did everything perfectly, but eventually had to radio in because they couldn't find one flag

– they expected it to be on the tree right in front of them, and it wasn't. When they were told to look up and they saw the flag just three feet above them, they felt pretty stupid.

That's why, if you were tracking me, I'd probably just climb a tree. But, if I were tracking you and you climbed a tree, I'd congratulate you on getting away from the bears, but I'd find your tracks towards the bottom of the tree and ride a big circle around it. If your tracks didn't continue in some direction, I'd come back and look up (if I hadn't already) – and you'd be hooped.

Aside from not looking up, there is another way that trackers can sabotage themselves: through preconceptions.

Preconceptions

Preconceptions include inventing tracks, because you know there has to be one, or being so focussed on what you're looking for that you miss what's staring you in the face.

If you're a bird watcher, focussing on what's flitting around in the trees, you probably don't see a lot of deer. Similarly, the tracker who focuses too much on footprints may miss important top sign like fabric on a branch, or something hanging in a tree. When most people find a coat in the bush, they think: "Oh, somebody dropped this or forgot their jacket," whereas a tracker is probably thinking: "Perhaps a lost soul has hypothermia and has started to shed clothing." Or when a child goes missing, police often think abduction (because it is their job to cover all the bases), where SAR volunteers are thinking that the kid wandered off. From these examples, you can see how different preconceptions could have you looking at the same situation very differently.

Preconceptions can truly be your worst enemy. They can waste you a lot of time or lose you the catch. You might follow inconclusive tracks for quite some time before you realize you were following the wrong quarry. You also have to fight the urge to make up sign or tracks. When you've been tracking for a while, and you're tired and have eye strain, you will likely invent a track or sign because you really want it to be there. This also happens when you lose the trail on a gravel road; you'll go on anything, like a broken twig or displaced rock, because you don't want to admit to yourself that you may have lost the trail.

If you're tired or discouraged, you have to slow down, trust yourself and trust the tracks, until you actually find the next sign. Really, at this point, you should take a break, rest your eyes and your mind, and consider focusing on how your other senses can help you track.

Chapter 6:
Sensory tracking

"All our knowledge begins with the senses, proceeds then to the understanding, and ends with reason."

Immanuel Kant

Trackers tend to focus mainly on visual sign, but there are ways to track using your other senses. You have to be open to everything your senses are telling you, and pay attention to those details. You might see a track, hear a branch snap, or smell musk or perfume, and all of these cues could help you find your prey.

Of course visual tracking is by far the most common, but it's worth noting how your other senses can help you in tracking as well.

Hearing

Is hearing a noise in the bush considered sign? Sure, someone tromping through the bush like a herd of elephants is changing the sounds of the woods, and so should also be considered sign. Following a noise is called auditory tracking.

People make a lot of noise even when they think they are being quiet. Listening for talking, footfalls, branches snapping, knuckle-cracking, and gum-smacking can help you hone in on your prey. People also aren't aware how loud their clothing can be. The zzzzzzzzttttt of Gore-Tex or nylon wind pants/jackets rubbing against itself or trees, not to mention opening up a jacket closed with Velcro, can wake the forest. A lot of the recommended material that keeps you dry is noisy.

Voices will also travel a long way. At certain times of day, and depending on the weather conditions and landscape, you can hear people talking 300 yards away. I've even heard people on the top of a ridge a quarter-mile away talking like they were right beside me. I don't pretend to understand the physics of it, but I do know it happens, and rarely on a sunny day, or a real gusty day. Overcast, calm days with a light breeze seem to carry noise the farthest.

Our hearing isn't all that good (compared to that of animals), so a lot of people instinctively cup their hand up to their ear when they are straining to hear something, using their hand to make their ear bigger to catch more sound waves. I can't say it's something I do, because while it may help you hear something, it doesn't really help you locate where the sound came from. When trying to locate sound, humans (or anything with two ears) will instinctively turn towards the noise, until the sound is in stereo (hitting both ears at the same time). Barn owls even have their ears set asymmetrically so that the difference in the time that it takes for the sound to get to each ear (just a fraction of a second) helps them pinpoint the noise. Their ears are also surrounded by feathers to focus sound into them. Many owls look like they have two satellite dishes on their faces with their eyes in the middle – and in a way they do. The facial feather ruff helps them to see better and to bounce sound into their ears. Ever wonder why a satellite dish is the shape that it is? The idea there is that no matter from what angle the sound comes in, it bounces to the middle. I suppose if we wanted to use this theory ourselves, we'd cup a hand to each ear, or just use some conical or dish-like listening device.

I've been asked why I don't just use special sound-enhancing technologies so that I could hear my prey talking and hone in on their direction easily. While the thought is good, the woods are not quiet places, so the sound magnifier would need to enhance noises selectively. You don't want to amplify crickets and birds chirping, or wind rubbing branches together, or squirrels chatting. Good luck trying to figure out if you should try to enhance the sound of branches or twigs snapping in the distance, as there is no way of knowing if it is your prey or a moose making the noise.

Auditory tracking is also tricky when echoes factor in, like when you're in a valley. Sometimes it is hard to know where the noise is actually coming from. If you've got your horse there or if there's an owl you can see in a tree, they aren't fooled by much and have a better sense of hearing: watch their head for the actual direction of sound.

There's a Bruce Cockburn song that goes: "If a tree falls in the forest does anybody hear?" Well if you weren't there when it fell, nobody heard it, and the only sign will be the uprooted tree. There's nothing to follow based on past noise that you didn't hear, but there might be something to follow if a past smell hasn't dissipated.

Smell

If you smell perfume, bad body odour, or smoke is that sign? Absolutely. The prey has left something behind. Even if you can't see it, you can follow it and find your prey. It's called scent tracking, most often done by dogs, but also doable by humans (but not as well) when the stink is strong.

You can pick up on strong odours from people's bodies, their excretions, smoke or cooking smells, freshly overturned dirt, or disturbed vegetation. Think of when you brush against cedar or pine in the forest: the smell intensifies and hangs in the air for a while. If you're cooking fish, or you sit around a campfire for a while, you also walk away smelling like fish or smoke.

Ever smell a ferret? They're stinky little buggers and have some pungent oil. Bears can have a real funny smell, wet and greasy; other times they don't smell at all. Their stink also changes based on how recently they've rolled in a dead animal. A buck also has a strong musky smell when in the **rut**.

If a tracker has a good sniffer, they may indeed be able to smell their prey. Like wine experts who detect blackberries and a hint of cigar in their red wine, you can train your nose to pick up scents in the woods.

In cooler, more humid weather, I've found that scents linger longer than in windy or hot days, but they can still be followed, or at least help you confirm other signs. My Uncle Jerry always said that when he'd cut up apples to draw in deer, he could smell the apples from quite a distance away when the cooler air was coming down, settling in and pushing the smell outwards.

Scents can definitely help with tracking. If you come across the smell of smoke you can follow it to a campfire site. Then you can hold your hand over the remains of the campfire, using your sense of touch to feel for warmth.

Touch

Touch tracking is sometimes used at night or in dark conditions, or if you have lost your sight (like from snow blindness). You won't see me crawling around on my hands and knees feeling for the next track! It would take too long to cover too small an area, which you could cover in minutes the next morning.

That said, I do touch sign to age it. Mud or dirt that has transferred to a leaf that is now dry and crumbly is older than mud that is still wet or dirt that holds a shape when you squish it between your fingers. If the edges of tracks crumble like sand to the touch, they're older than ones that break off in small pieces. Tracks frozen into the ground that are rock hard when touched tell me they were there before the freeze.

Mud has been transferred forward to this moss on a rock. Picking it up and seeing if it crumbles or holds its shape helps you to age it.

I'll also hold my hand over ashes or coals to feel for heat to determine the age of a fire, and I've touched a candy or granola bar wrapper to see if it's still sticky, which means it's fairly fresh.

So, while you won't see me using touch tracking for directionality, it can be helpful in aging a sign.

Taste

The fifth sense, taste, just doesn't come into tracking, unless you pass a wild blueberry patch and want a snack. If you meet someone who tells you they can lick a tree or the ground and tell you what animals have passed by recently, smile and nod, and then go find someone sane to talk with.

Sixth sense

Sometimes people talk about a sixth sense: intuition. Intuition in tracking, to me, is taking what you know and making inferences about behaviour (of man or beast). There's always some guesswork in tracking, but typically they're educated guesses, based on knowing your prey and the terrain, and reasoning things through. You ask yourself, "If I were them, what would I do here? What has their pattern so far shown me that they might do?" Some people say "Let your intuition guide you," but I think it's really "Let your experience guide you." You use most of your senses and all of your faculties of knowledge and reason to find the first track, and the next, and the next, to determine what you want to know.

When in doubt, try not to overanalyze or let negative thoughts creep in; just look for the next track or sign. You have to trust the signs, trust yourself, and trust the track. How can you trust a track? It's probably worthwhile explaining a little more about what a track can tell you.

Chapter 7:
What's a track and what can it tell you?

"I've got him...tracks are closer together...he's slowing down...It's heading North...its tracks are still fresh."

Cowboys & Aliens (2011 Sci-fi Western movie)

A **track** is a footprint, paw print, or hoof print, and it's an example of ground sign.

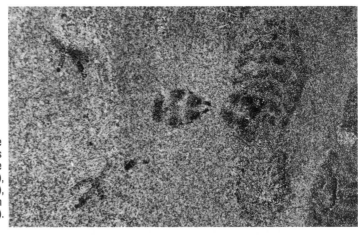

There are three types of tracks in this one photo: bird (left), coyote (middle), and human (right).

A track can be **conclusive sign** (sign definitely from the prey we seek) or **corroborating sign** (sign that isn't conclusively from our prey but that supports other sign).

Unless photographers, hunters, and/or conservationists are seeking a specific animal (one that is wounded, known to be aggressive towards humans, or a prize-size animal), they don't much care if sign is conclusive, because they would be just as happy with any deer, and not the deer they started tracking. But when you're tracking people in Search and Rescue, you're looking for conclusively human sign, like a boot print, and specifically one particular tread pattern.

Sometimes you might see a scuff mark, and then some shine, and later down the road, on softer ground, the shine turns into coyote tracks. The lingo then would be that the scuff mark and shine could be called corroborating sign. If you weren't looking for coyote, you're going to have to go back to the last known conclusive sign, and start again from there.

I think it goes without saying that you can't expect to see a beautiful trail of complete footprint impressions that lead right to your prey. It rarely if ever happens, and if you do get a nice trail, it's usually only for a few feet.

When looking at a track, there is a lot to learn from it. As you may have heard me say, "Interpretation is 90%." A track can give you information on the size, weight, and footwear of the prey, their direction of travel, speed of travel, time of travel, and physical condition. Always think to yourself, "What is this track telling me? What is this pattern of tracks telling me?" Get a feel for the track and the context of each track. You start with the track, then look at/for the trail, and always consider both within the overall context or terrain.

A lot of this is common sense, but if you haven't thought about it much, this quick list can get you thinking or act as a reminder. Here are some things you can learn from a track in the same type of terrain, the most obvious listed first:

- *Tracks from a high heel look very different from hiking boot tracks*
- *The smaller the track, the smaller the foot*
- *The deeper the track, the heavier the prey*
- *The wider apart the tracks, the longer the prey's legs and/or the faster the prey is moving*
- *The crisper the tracks, the more recent they are.*

The adult's step is the equivalent of two steps of the child. Children also tend to drag their feet more.

Overall, when I'm looking at a track, the first thing I want to make sure of is that I'm looking at the right track. Then I figure out direction, so that I know where to look for the next track. On top of direction, I'm also thinking about the speed of travel, to determine how far away the next track will be. Then I'm thinking about when they were here, and what their physical and emotional condition was. One track won't tell you that; you need a trail to figure that out. Regardless, I always start by identifying my prey.

Identifying your prey

Before you start following any set of tracks, you want to be following the right ones. If you're looking for a stray cow, don't follow the moose tracks. If you're looking for a lost child, don't follow the tracks of a 300-pound adult hiker. So the size and depth of tracks is important.

Like I said before, you can measure track size using a tracking stick, by marking the size of the track and step with different colour elastics on the stick. That way, when you're looking for the next track in a series, you can hold your tracking stick at the marking for the step and move the stick in an arc outwards from the last track to find more sign, even if a track isn't there. The end of the stick should be the location of the next track or sign, even if it's just a negative imprint from a kicked stone.

Specific to human tracks, looking at the pattern of the tread from their footwear can help you to determine if it's the correct set of tracks to follow. Tread patterns often have patterns of lines, curves, swirls, or geometric shapes. Identifying unique markings and looking for those in subsequent tracks could help lead you to your quarry. (As I mentioned before, I tracked one girl for the better part of two days based on three distinctive lines in the back of her heel print).

Even if I didn't have the full track below it, the partial print I'm pointing at (look closely) shows four tell-tale dots of the prey's footwear tread: conclusive sign of the prey I'm tracking.

Also good to remember is that everyone walks differently, so the wear on the inside or the outside of the sole will be different, and that also shows up in the tracks and helps you identify a track conclusively.

Direction and speed of travel

Clues to the direction, the speed of travel and the prey's state of mind are all available in a set of tracks. Straight tracks show they're focused and on a mission. If the tracks turn (one foot goes sideways, or a foot every few paces is pointed 45 degrees), they're looking behind them every so often and are possibly nervous, or scared, or trying not to get lost.

About now, some more terminology would be helpful to make things as clear as mud:

- **Step** *is the distance between the heel of one track and the heel of the next track*
- **Stride** *is the distance between the heel of a right foot track and the heel of the next right foot track (it's the length of two steps)*
- **Straddle** *is the distance between the inside of the right and left tracks*
- **Pitch** *is the distance/angle off centre that a track is angled*
- **Directionality** *is the direction of travel. It's as easy as following the direction of the toe of the track (except, of course, if human prey is trying to evade you).*

Applying these terms, when your prey is walking backwards, the step and stride are usually shorter, pitch is greater, and straddle is irregular too. The step and stride are longer when the **gait** (or speed of travel) is faster.

Walking backwards (left); walking forwards (right). Notice the difference in the length of the step, and the pitch.

Toe kicks or heel strikes also indicate directionality, so I'll talk about those next.

A **toe kick** is the dirt plume left from a person's toes pushing off the ground to move forwards. This happens because most people walk heel to toe. The heel goes down first, then the toes, and the toe of their shoe or boot scratches dirt backwards as they push off the ground to move their foot forwards. As the toe gives that last flick in a step, the dirt is moved backwards, opposite to the direction of travel.

The toe kick is seen here in the front couple inches of the track: the ground is pushed in further and there is a small pile up of dirt in the track, about an inch from the front of the track.

A **heel strike** is that first imprint made by your heel when you take a step. In soft dirt, the first edge of a heel strike is deeper than the rest of the track (unless the person was walking backwards).

Notice how dark the shadow is in the heel because the heel strike is deeper.

Someone running has very little, if any, heel strike, whereas walking has definite heel strikes and toe kicks. There are no toe kicks when someone is walking backwards.

There are a few exceptions or additional notes to add here. If you're walking in deep snow or mud, your toe comes up through the snow/mud in front of your foot and can send the snow/mud forwards. It's not a toe kick, it's just the snow/mud sprayed forward in the direction of travel.

Can you tell which person is walking forwards and which is walking backwards? (Hint: walking backwards there is no dragging of the feet). Also notice the snow sprayed forward in front of the set of tracks on the left (nice and visible in front of the first track of the right foot).

Wet versus dry leaves also act differently, and of course, travelling up or downhill is different, as well. For example, if you're travelling uphill, wet leaves will pile up at the back of the track.

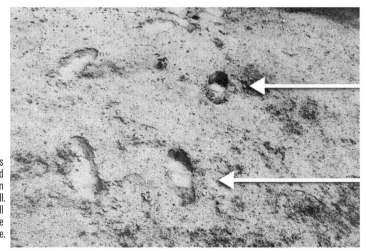

Someone has walked up and back down this sandy hill. Walking downhill you see more heel strike.

Also, if someone is walking backwards, you won't see toe kicks, but there is often a drag. If the person isn't lifting his or her feet on purpose, the toes strike first and the heel drags backwards, pulling dirt or snow into the direction of travel.

This is not toe kick – this is snow dragged from someone walking backwards that didn't lift their feet much.

We'll look at backwards walking and other evasive manoeuvres a bit later.

An interesting fact for cloven hoofed animals (like moose and deer) is that their toes spread apart for better grip or traction when they run. So if the individual track is splayed open with a decent ridge between the toes, you know they were travelling at a good clip, and could be quite a distance away from you.

This deer was moving a good clip: its toes are spread open.

Even with humans, you need to be prepared for a change in gait. The step and stride will get longer if the prey breaks into a run, and you'll usually get a more definitive track and bigger toe kick where they broke into a different stride.

Once you have a track identified as the one you're tracking, you have to find the next track. You try to anticipate the next track location from the pattern already presented. If you can't find the track, scan ahead to where you think the next track or sign should be. If nothing's there, scan the sides of the path for exit tracks. If there is none, take a couple more paces to pick up a track, but if there is still nothing, go back to last known track and start again. As mentioned, you can use a tracking stick to measure the step or stride and look for the next track (or more subtle sign) within that radius. And of course, avoid walking in tracks – you'd be surprised at how often this happens.

Direction of travel isn't visible only in the tracks, vegetation also gives sign to help you along the way. For example, tall grass stays down pointing out the direction of travel (I'll come back to this a bit later in relation to vegetation disturbances).

The grass is pushed down in the direction of travel, here the disturbed vegetation acts like a pointer to where they went.

So far, direction of travel and speed are part of the story that a track or trail of tracks can tell you, but knowing *when* someone went through an area is really important, too.

Aging: time of travel

Aging a track involves reading the ground. It has to do with checking things like moisture, or the lack of it, and evaluating the depth, crispness, and amount of erosion.

Aging a track will help you determine how far ahead the prey may be. Here's a few things to consider when aging a track (you've already read a few under "Touch Tracking" but they're worth repeating here):

- *New tracks have defined, square edges. They round with age.*
- *If the edges of tracks crumble like sand to the touch, they're older than ones where you can break off a small piece.*
- *Tracks frozen into the ground that are rock hard when touched tell me they were there before the freeze (which is only really helpful information if you're tracking something around the time of the first freeze). Ground that freezes is highly deceiving, especially if protected by a rock or some weather barrier – a track can last in near perfect condition all winter.*

- *The consistency/type of soil, and the weather, determine how long the track will last.*
- *When looking at tracks that appear fresh, but then stop and are hidden by snow, if you knew the weather, you could figure out that the tracks had to be at least as old as a minute before the last snowfall.*
- *Full prints are easier to age: they have more definition to start, so you'll notice more degradation with time.*
- *Mud or dirt that has transferred to a leaf and is now dry is older than mud that is still wet or dirt that holds a shape when you squish it between your fingers.*

You can see that this track is several hours old by how the dirt has dried out and has turned white. The white dirt is crumbly like sand.

Aging can also be applied to more than just a track. Like we mentioned in touch tracking, you can age a campfire by the warmth coming off the remains of it. I've heard people say they can also age a "bed" in the grass by warmth, but I'm not convinced. I've jumped animals out of their beds but there is no residual heat there – because deer and moose have hollow hair. A person loses a lot more heat, so maybe their bum-print will still be warm if they just left. But since I don't track with an infrared camera or glasses, I don't really use this method.

There isn't a lot of brown on this apple, so the person who ate it isn't too far ahead.

Aging scat takes more specific knowledge of your prey. From experience, I know that if it's cold out and you're tracking deer, shiny piles of scat are fresher than dull-coloured stuff. Other than that, I can tell you for sure that if you come across bear scat and it's still steaming, you might want to back up a little.

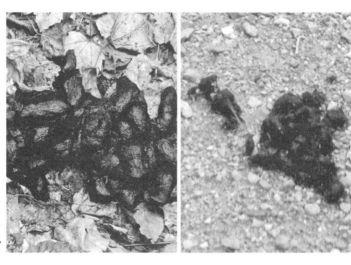

Fresh, shiny moose scat and older, duller bear scat.

For aging vegetation, if prey has walked on a plant and crushed it on a rock before the plant rebounds, there will be bruising on the plant. Fresh bruising starts off darker green than the leaf, on the back of the leaf. As time passes, the bruised area starts to turn yellow or brown and dries out. The bruising will eventually go through to the front of the leaf as it dries out. If you're stuck for sign, start flipping over leaves to see if there is any bruising, as it will show on the underside of the leaf first.

The leaf in the first photo shows no sign of being stepped on, but once flipped over, the damage from being stepped on is clear.

Physical condition

Tracks and sign can also give us information about the physical condition of the prey. When people are tired, or carrying a heavy load, they tend to drag their feet more. Or, you may see long drag marks from a limp, suggesting an ankle, leg, or hip injury. There may be stick holes in the ground if someone has fashioned crutches or a cane for themselves (again, perhaps for an ankle, leg, or hip injury?).

The limp of this person's right leg makes you wonder if they have injured their ankle, knee, or hip.

On the flip side, if you see knee impressions in the ground by a creek where someone has probably stopped to take a drink, their knees, hips, and legs are okay. If you continue to notice snapped twigs on trees, at least one arm is ok. If the tracks show you that they stepped over a log, then their back and legs are ok.

Perhaps the most obvious indicator of poor physical condition may be the additional sign they leave behind in terms of blood (drops or smears). Tracking someone wounded who doesn't want to be found is pretty much in a wreck, as they'll leave more sign. Tired or careless walking leaves drag marks and more ground sign, and typically breaks more branches. Injuries where the skin is broken leave blood transfer on trees, or a trail of droplets to follow on the ground.

Prove it!

To learn about the aging of tracks, or to figure out what a track is telling you, there aren't a lot of shortcuts. The best way to learn is to make your own tracks and label them (some in the sun, some in the shade), check them every one to four hours (make four or five tracks every couple of hours), take photos each time, and then flip through the photos on your camera or phone to compare what happens. You can make a kind of test bed for tracks and replicate your trails in the fall, winter, spring, and summer. Keep track of the weather, and wind, to note any changes. Truly, the only way to get better is to do it and see it for yourself: it's a long, slow process.

Tracks in the shade (top left) last longer than those melted by the sun (top right). Marking the time beside tracks helps you learn aging (right).

For any of these things you've just read, you don't have to believe me. Try them for yourself.

- *Step on a leaf on top of a rock. Look at it: see how the bruised area is wet and darker on the backside of the leaf. Then come back every couple of hours and look at it again. See how long it takes to show yellowing and browning.*
- *Step in some soil. Look at the crisp track you leave, go back every couple of hours and see how wind and sun affected the edges and ridges of the track. Repeat this in sunny and shady conditions, in a wind-protected area, and in the open.*

Also, try to replicate a track that you don't understand. Is there a drag on one side? Perhaps the prey was limping. Is there an arc? The prey may have turned abruptly.

Every step we take, we leave evidence of being there, but some is really hard to see. Every track has a story to tell. You just have to figure out what the story is. You see an animal or a person do something, then you go look at the tracks. You create a log in your head of what tracks mean. If you see human tracks you don't understand, try to recreate them until you know what they mean and how they were made.

The tracks tell a story of a person walking forwards, turning, looking right and then back, and then continuing to walk.

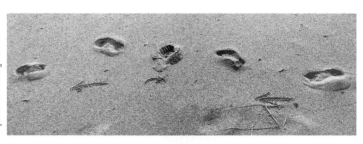

Go into the woods and look for examples of all of the groupings of sign that I listed for you on page 15 under "Tracking and sign awareness" but don't be surprised or discouraged if you don't see anything right off – no one does, really. At the beginning of every season, I get out into the bush to get my eyes used to looking at the ground again.

Look for ground impressions. Aside from the obvious foot impressions, or tracks, can you see where someone was sitting or an animal was sleeping? Find a transfer – is there mud on the rock where a hiker stepped out of a puddle? Are there water droplets showing the direction of your prey's travel leaving a stream? Is there obvious damage to the environment? Did a deer nibble some bushes or a bear eat some blueberries? Are there remnants of a campfire on the ground? Look for disturbances – did someone kick a rock out of place and leave a divot? Is the grass pressed down and shimmering silver in the sunlight? Did your prey leave something behind? Did clothing or fur get snagged on a twig, or did the prey litter? Is there fresh scat on the trail?

Top row: coyote tracks (impressions); a watery boot print on a rock (transfers); the negative imprint from a rock kicked out of place (disturbances) Bottom row: charred earth from a fire pit (damage); and a discarded water bottle (things left behind)

If you don't have a lot of wilderness around you, that's ok, too. You can do test beds on your lawn or driveway in the winter. You can walk through a puddle in the summer and see how long the water transfer takes to evaporate. You can have someone walk across your lawn and observe the direction of travel by the path left in the grass.

Did the mailperson walk towards you or away from you across the grass? Look at page 88-89, "Tracking in different conditions: Through vegetation" for the answer!

All that said, I don't recommend that you do any tracking in your house. Testing mud transfer from your muddy boots across the kitchen mat and floor will only show you how well the person who cleans the house can track you down. When they find you, they won't be applauding you for your new tracking skills – you'll probably be handed a mop and you'll only learn how to erase your tracks [wink].

I'm hoping this book's descriptions and photos will help you to get out and practice and see what you may not have noticed before. (But I acknowledge that the best way to learn is to have an experienced tracker point out sign as you go – maybe I'll see you in one of my courses sometime). Trackers aren't born: you will only learn by doing. So, next are some of the main skills of a tracker that you can practice.

Chapter 8:
Learning to track: skills of a tracker

"Experience is one thing you can't get for nothing."

Oscar Wilde

"The Beauty of the Mountain is hidden for all those who try to discover it from the top, supposing that, one way or an other, one can reach this place directly. The Beauty of the Mountain reveals only to those who climbed it."

Antoine de Saint-Exupéry

Anyone with decent powers of observation and a willingness to spend time in the bush learning can pick up the basics of tracking. Knowing about animal and human behaviour, as well as animals' habitats, is helpful. Reading can be a good jumpstart, but there is no substitute for spending time in the bush, paying attention to what you're stepping on. There you can make your own tracks and see how they age. You can observe tracks being made first-hand by animals and others, and then go and look at the tracks. Before getting into reading sign, there are a few skills that make for a good tracker, so let's start there.

Tracking has its roots in basic human survival. Without tracking, we couldn't have avoided predators or found prey. Today, finding food is as easy as driving to the nearest grocery store, armed with a credit card, but go back even a hundred years, and we went into the bush armed with a bow, slingshot, spear, or gun.

Early trackers were armed with much more than weapons: they also had finely-tuned tracking skills, including a knowledge of their prey and their prey's habitats. They knew they didn't have the physical prowess of most of their prey, so they had to outsmart them. They were physically fit, patient, present, persistent, positive, they paid attention and problem-solved, were prepared, and part of their surroundings. Now, let's look at each of those attributes individually.

Physical fitness

You have to be able to keep up with your prey, whether you're riding a horse or not. Search and Rescue can be really exhausting, and you need the mental and physical stamina to be able to see the operation through to finding the lost person. You need to be able to cover the terrain that your prey did, and catch up with them, which means you have to do it faster than they did. You have to be in good shape to track successfully.

That said, the idea of me preaching physical fitness is a bit funny, because I don't go to the gym. I've found that there are all kinds of good ways to work up a sweat without ever seeing the inside of a gym. Many of them involve good, honest, hard work. As a cowboy, you put in long hours haying, fencing, roping, and doing any other chore thrown at you that day – you're not just sitting on the back of a horse like a bump on a log. At cookhouses, dinner is made for you, but you learn pretty fast to be courteous and bring your dishes back to the kitchen – so part of my daily exercise since my start in ranching has always been to walk my plate to the sink [wink].

Whether I'm ranching, tilling a garden, or doing my carpentry work, I'm staying fit without aiming to do so. You may have heard me say it before, and I'll say it again – I love a good walk as long as there's a horse between my legs.

Patience

If you expect to find full footprints every time you track, showing you a perfect trail that will lead you right to your prey, you will be sorely disappointed. Tracking takes time. If you don't go slowly, and find all of the relevant sign, you will often have to circle back and start again. You have to be patient and check your assumptions along the way. Moving too quickly can cost you valuable time later on. It's like the tortoise and the hare: slow and steady wins the race.

The other side of patience is waiting for the other person or animal to make a mistake. If you can outwait them, you can often outsmart them.

There have been times that I've been tracking, and my horse has heard something in the bush, so I stopped and waited for a minute or so, but I got impatient and left. If I'd waited just a bit longer, I could have caught the prey right there – but we live and we learn.

Life is fast nowadays, and people in deadline-driven careers often don't know how to do things slowly. Just remember that there are things in life that are worth waiting for. If you're rushing through life, stop and ask yourself, what's the rush? Your ultimate destination is a pine box, so why hurry to get to it? Slow down. Relax.

Try this: set a timer for three minutes and sit down and do nothing. The first time you do it, you may need to have a pen and paper beside you to write down all the things you realize you have to get done and you aren't doing while you're sitting there. That's ok. After you write down your to-do list, reset the timer and try again. Take it slow, maybe start the timer with one minute and work your way up. Stare out the window, look at the trees, look around the trees: take the time to see things that you don't normally look for.

Try being still in the woods too. Find a spot and sit there for a good spell (don't bring a timer). Just look, listen, and smell. What have you learned about your surroundings by taking the time to stop and look?

Go for a walk in a ten-foot-square area. Like the motorcycle race from one side of the road to the other, the last one that gets across the road wins (it's harder to go slower). See what you can notice by moving slowly in a small area, focusing on every step. You'll probably notice how noisy you are in your movements. Slow them down and get quieter, as it will help in your tracking.

Some of us come by patience more easily, depending on how we were raised and what we do for a living. As I was growing up, the ranchers and farmers I worked for taught me that you may as well do a job right the first time so you don't have to do it again. I wasn't often told to redo things, but I've seen fresh guys come in and patch up a fence in a hurry, and then have to go back to fix it properly later – usually in the rain or snow.

And like I said before, tearing down a bunch of houses, board by board, with my stepdad was an exercise in patience (or frustration, depending on who you asked). Raised by my mom and having three sisters, if I ever wanted to see the inside of a bathroom, I had no choice but to be patient.

I'm a pretty patient guy, but no one is perfect. I find myself getting cranky with stupid drivers. The guy who does ten under the speed limit, the guy who stops before he merges – that's why they don't let people like me pack rifles while driving [wink].

You can probably see by now why patience is so important in tracking. You have to take the time to find the missing tracks or the hard-to-find tracks. If you jump ahead too quickly, you'll have to turn back and you may disturb the actual tracks. Sometimes, you've got to go very slow to go very fast.

Be present

Ever tried to remember a list of items to buy at the grocery store when you're mad at your sweetie for making you go to the store in the first place? It doesn't work very well. Maybe you attempted my patience exercise and tried to sit still for three minutes and couldn't even make it to one minute because you remembered you had the laundry to fold and the dishwasher to run. When you were a student, how much of your math lesson did you remember when you were busy daydreaming about the party that weekend? You just weren't "there." For tracking, you have to be *all* there, mentally and physically. Same way you shouldn't be thinking about your evening plans when your honey is telling you about her day, you can't be thinking about work deadlines when you're out tracking a lost child. You need to be connected or you'll miss something.

Part of being present is being aware of the time of day, the weather, and your surroundings. The easiest track to lose is often track of time. Pay attention to the time of day, using a watch or the sun's position. Make sure you're ready to camp for the night and navigate in the dark, or head home before it gets too dark.

Also be on the lookout for changes in the weather, since weather can come in fast. Are clouds moving in? Is there a sudden change in temperature? Is the wind strong? Most of the hunters in Alberta who get lost do so because of a condition called an "upslope event." It's like a washing machine, tossing heavy snow up against the mountains in a hurry. Suddenly, you can't see squat, you're in two feet of snow, and all of the tracks that might have been there to help SAR find you are gone. Fog also changes everything. For one, you always think you've gone farther in the fog than you actually have.

Persistence

Tracking isn't always fun. The weather can be a real bugger, and so can the terrain. Or the people you're tracking alongside can be a real pain. You also aren't going to learn the skills overnight. You need to be persistent and practice tracking; you need to persevere through tough conditions.

The challenge or goal keeps me going. My reward is finding the feet still in the tracks. Especially in Search and Rescue, you don't give up without a real good reason. You stay focused on your prey, their tracks, and the trail. If the trail goes missing, you have to be persistent and go back to that last-known track, then use a search pattern to find the next sign. Unless your prey can suddenly go airborne, there will be more sign. You just have to persevere until you find it, and hope that you haven't obliterated it yourself. If the bugs are bad, use bug spray (we'll get to preparedness in a few pages, but it's fair to say that it's hard to persist through tough conditions when you're not prepared for them).

Let's face it, most of the best things in life don't come easy. Very few things worth having in life are just handed to us. There is a lot of work behind every "overnight sensation." Persistence will get you closer to your goal.

In the face of challenges, focus on the feeling of achievement from succeeding, not the current setback. When you're thrown from a horse, you don't quit being a cowboy. You pick yourself up, dust yourself off, and get back on the horse.

Positive attitude

I think it was Henry Ford who said, "Whether you think you can or you think you can't – you're right." If you think that there's no way you will find your prey, you're right. If you think the weather or other searchers have obliterated the trail, you're right. If you think it's too cold or too wet to continue, you're going to be right. In roping, if you need to pick up the heels of the cow, don't talk yourself out of it before you even toss the rope.

Before tracking, I avoid having a preconceived notion of how it might end, because expectations can play out. If you think the country is going to be really tough, you'll find it tough. I don't like negative thoughts – they don't add much to life. I'd probably go so far as to say that I don't deal well with negativity. If I say I'm going to call Brian, and someone says "he's probably not home," that's just negative and I don't need it.

I should mention that sometimes negative thoughts are there to warn you of imminent danger, so listen to your gut instincts. For the most part, though, it's just a negative outlook creeping in for no good reason, so slam the door on it. Griping about something for hours on end to anyone who'll listen won't make the work go any faster. Use the energy you would typically waste on complaining to start the job with a "git 'er done" attitude.

That's one good trait about most cowboys: we might be shivering to death, with rain sneaking down our slicker while we're five miles from home, but you won't hear cowboys moaning and groaning much. What's more likely is that one of you might say: "Weather's not all that great." And the other cowboy would snort back with a smile: "Yup, the weather can smarten up any damn time it wants," and you'd get back to finishing the task at hand so that you could ride home and warm up. We've got pretty good senses of humour, and are never short on jokes, puns, innuendo, one-liners, and a healthy dose of sarcasm to keep things light.

You've got to be positive. No matter what you're doing, find the good in it, even in the rotten jobs you're doing. Don't forget to look around and smell the flowers, because life can get pretty crappy sometimes. And not to get all philosophical, but I also don't waste a lot of time on regrets, or you'll miss out in the present.

Pay attention to detail

I really can't say enough about this one. You can't expect to get much out of life if you aren't paying attention to what's going on around you. Whether you're tracking a wounded bear, or walk into a room and notice your sweetie is acting like a wounded bear, you have to pay attention to the subtle and not so subtle cues around you.

What can you do to solve the mystery? You need data. You need one sign to start with and work backwards or forwards from there. Missing the fact that you just walked through a full cobweb, even though you were only an hour behind the prey, should have told you to turn around, that you were going the wrong way, because spiders just don't spin that fast. Missing the fact that today your sweetie is sporting a new hair-do, especially after she talked about going to the salon that day at breakfast, should have told you to turn around and go buy flowers. [wink]

More applicable to tracking, but similar, remembering what the weather was like for the past few days will help you age tracks. Remembering what tracks looked like in your earlier experiences will also go a long way in the field. In addition to remembering details about the track you're looking for, you also have to be paying attention to the time of day, weather, and path behind you to know how to get out later.

To work your memory and skills in paying attention to detail, there are lots of things you can do. You might start by not programming people's numbers into your telephone and instead remembering them on your own. Or, when you're at a table of friends at a restaurant, listen to what everyone is ordering and see if you can remember the whole order.

At home, you can grab a deck of cards and play concentration. You can look up the exact rules, but from what I remember, you take all of the red or black cards and put them aside (it's easier to start with 26 cards than 52). Line up the cards, face down, (this could be five rows of five and one at the side, or two rows of 13). Now flip over any two cards and try to find pairs of cards that match (two fives, or two queens, etc.). If there's no match, put them face down again. If there is a match, take them out, put them in a pile and flip over two more cards. The key of course is in remembering the cards that weren't a match for future picks. It's not easy at first, but you'll get better with practice, and you'll be keeping your brain healthy too.

Another game is to grab around 20 different small items like a paperclip, pushpin, pen, mint, match book, pebble, watch, etc. Put them on top of a plain cloth napkin. Study the items for 30 seconds and then have them taken away or fold up the napkin. Write down all of the items that you remember. Some people call this it Kim's game. Keep practicing and your recall will improve. You can make this more difficult by adding more items, or by shortening the time you have to study them.

The more you do this, the more you'll be able to see the image of those items on your eyes once you look away (look back at the section about "Reading what's 'on' your eyes" if you've forgotten). Sometimes, the longer you look at something, the less you notice overall, because you start getting caught up in specifics. Back in the bush, this can happen when there is a tree that is predominant in your sight line. You're scanning the area, but you keep coming back to that tree. You follow it up and look at the branches, then you notice the moss on the tree at the base. Then you realize you've stopped scanning the landscape, and you've missed catching a glimpse of a deer behind the deadfall that you might well have noticed if you'd just scanned back and forth.

Sometimes, though, you want to remember details, like the tread pattern on the sole of a shoe. Your detail recall can be honed too. There used to be a test similar to what I am going to explain next in the application process for the RCMP (I'm not sure if they still use it). It's based on witnesses being asked to remember what they saw surrounding a crime. Eyewitnesses are notoriously bad at this by the way, and make a lot of false judgments, but the skill can be trained.

Open a magazine and find an advertisement or photo with several people or animals in the foreground and background. Spend a minute studying the photo and then close the book and write down everything you can remember about the photo. Make it more challenging by giving yourself less time, or by asking someone to quiz you about the photo. Questions can be about anything: How many people were in the photo? What time was it on the clock? Was anyone wearing a blue shirt? Who was holding the hammer? What colour were the walls of the house? I do this sometimes when I'm waiting at a doctor's office and I'm not interested in reading any of the old magazines lying about.

I've been asked before if my tracking attention to detail and patience also flows into my personal life. In my carpentry, for sure, I take pride in what I do and spend a lot of time on detail work. I also do tend to notice when female friends change their hair colour and cut (which is a great skill to have – men take note). I can remember numbers easily, but names I'm not so good at. To help, I look them in the eye and say their name back to them as I shake their hand, and when I can, I write their name down and how I met them and where, or what they do. In a typical autograph session, with three hundred people, I'll remember one to three names, based on what they wore or said, because I associated their name to something. If I'm introduced to eight people at once...forget it (no pun intended).

Problem-solving

To be a good tracker, you have to like to solve problems. Sure, you have to be able to find the puzzle pieces, but you also have to want to put them together. You have to take in information from the sign or track in front of you, from the series of them, and factor in the environment and your knowledge of the area and prey. A row of footprints leading north does not mean the prey went north (unless they're animal tracks). Did you pay attention to the fact that there was a lot of drag at the heels and the prints were also deeper in the heels? Were the tracks closer together than the person's normal gait? If yes, they were walking backwards. Problem solved – start travelling south along those tracks.

Problem-solving involves storing data from before and applying it by using deduction and reasoning skills. This means you have to know what the puzzle pieces look like, and remember them. If you don't remember the difference between a cow and a moose track, how can you be sure you aren't leading people on a wild goose chase? Or should I say wild moose chase? [wink] Knowledge of tracks and memory skills are then part of preparedness for tracking.

Preparedness

Keeping on that example, imagine the big game guide who has a hunting group looking for moose but has been tracking a cow all day. Does the guide then turn and say, "Wow, that is one sickly moose: his rack has fallen off, and he's really stuck up to his knees in that mud, we'd best leave him alone, eh?" He wouldn't get a lot of repeat business when word got out. You have to know your prey!

Aside from knowing about tracks, having an understanding of your prey's routine is also a part of preparedness. If your prey is an animal, do you know what they eat, where they sleep, where they find their food and water, what their predators are, and what routes they often take? If your prey is human, do you know their age, weight, shoe size, sex, hobbies, levels of physical fitness and outdoors skills? What were the clothes they were last seen wearing?

A student of tracking is a student of human and animal behaviour and of the environment. You have to be able to think like what you track. The more you know about your prey the better you'll be able to get into their heads, helping you figure out what they may have done and where they may have gone.

Before you start a day of tracking, you should also be mentally and physically prepared. Be well-rested. Stay hydrated. Eat. Keep a positive attitude.

You also have to know the area. Get local maps (street maps, marked hiking/biking/horseback/motorized vehicle trail maps) and a topographic map of the area. A **topographical** or **topographic map** is a map that has contour lines that show elevation and depression of the surrounding landscape, and marks features of an area: water, vegetation, roads, highways, etc. Use these to help you understand where your prey might be headed. Leverage your map knowledge with local expertise and up-to-date information on common weather patterns, outdoors activities and landmarks in the area (hunting, hiking, etc.), and recent changes to the area (abandoned roads, abandoned cabins/shelters/caves/mines, wash-outs, construction, water springs, unmarked hiking trails, common local wilderness haunts, and dangers).

Topographic (**topo**) maps can also point out limitations of your prey's movement like large cliffs, rivers, or lakes that would impede progress, or paths of least resistance that they may travel (railroads, trails, old logging roads).

Now, there's no point having a topo map if you don't know how to read one. Same goes for a compass: know how to use one before you set out. Another handy preparedness tip is to remember to bring the map and compass with you: they aren't much good to you sitting at home on the kitchen counter – though if you had marked your route on it, at least it will make it easier for Search and Rescue (SAR) to find you should you get lost. If your map isn't waterproof, bring along a map bag or Ziploc bag to protect it from the weather and your handling of the map.

People always ask me if I use a GPS, but so far I still prefer a topo map and a compass (I've never had a map or compass run out of batteries). Remember that a standard GPS can tell you the way to a place, but not necessarily the best way. It's a marvelous tool, but it usually tells you the path as the crow flies, cutting across who knows what type of terrain, not necessarily taking advantage of the trails in the area that can save you time and energy. (I keep saying "not necessarily" because you have to have specific maps loaded on your GPS if you want to see contour lines and trails, but many old **skidder trails** (unused logging paths) aren't marked on a GPS). Yes, GPS is a good tool, to be used with your map and compass, but understand its limitations. It's great if your GPS combines your topographic map and compass in one, but it still goes without saying that you need to know how to use it, that you have spare batteries for it, and you also bring along weather protection for it (Ziploc bag).

Aside from protecting your map and GPS from the weather, you yourself have to make sure that you have the right gear for nasty weather. You may want some items with you to help you build shelter and/or stay warm (or cool). A good knife or small saw, fire starter, matches, a tarp, some rope, and an emergency blanket can go a long way if you need to spend the night in the bush. A headlamp and a signalling device (flare, mirror and light source) might also help you stay safe and get found. Layer your clothing, choose quick-dry fabrics, have a rain poncho or the like, a hat, and some extra socks.

Make sure your footwear is suitable for long walks and you've broken it in well (or bring moleskin for blisters). A digital camera is also nice to have to take photos of the trail behind you if you're worried you might not remember which path to take back. It can also be a big help to take photos of the track you're following to compare future tracks or partials on your camera screen later on.

In SAR, you're operating outside, and are required to be self-sufficient for a number of hours. Most searchers don't leave home without a 24-hour pack, no matter how fair the weather.

That pack always has extra food and water to sustain the searcher and one other person for 24 hours, basic first-aid supplies, sunscreen, bug spray, a cell phone that works in the bush, radios to communicate with base, and many of the items I've already listed above.

In case you want to refer back to this to help you prepare, here's a list that will let you navigate, be prepared for changes in weather and terrain, and have what you need to sustain yourself and someone else as well for 24-hours:

- ☐ *topographical map with trails marked, a compass, and a map bag (to keep it dry)*
- ☐ *watch*
- ☐ *layered clothing, quick-dry clothes, a fleece layer, extra socks, underwear, gloves, toque*
- ☐ *broken-in boots*
- ☐ *waterproof rain gear (a brightly coloured rain poncho or Gore-Tex jacket)*
- ☐ *food for 24 hours*
- ☐ *water for 24 hours − I recommend two water bladders and water treatment pills or gear*
- ☐ *light source (headlamp or flashlight), and spare batteries*
- ☐ *signalling device (flare, mirror) and a whistle*
- ☐ *sleeping gear (8x10 tarp and a space blanket for sure, but a ground pad and sleeping bag are nice-to-haves)*
- ☐ *ibuprofen (sleeping on the ground is no fun)*
- ☐ *small first-aid kit*
- ☐ *matches/fire starter for warmth and even cooking (a small pot and utensils are handy too)*
- ☐ *multi-tool, small folding saw, and/or good hunting knife*
- ☐ *bug spray, bear spray, sunscreen*
- ☐ *rope*
- ☐ *duct tape (it's just so handy in so many situations)*
- ☐ *cell phone, walkie-talkie*
- ☐ *SPOT Satellite GPS Messenger (more on this gadget later!)*
- ☐ *GPS, and spare batteries (nice to have − especially if there are topo maps loaded on it)*
- ☐ *toothbrush*
- ☐ *toilet paper*
- ☐ *sunglasses or some kind of eye protection. I don't wear them for tracking, but they would have been*

handy when a branch snapped back and hit me in the eye recently!

☐ *gaiters are nice to have to keep crap out of your boots and protect your shins if you know you'll be cutting through a lot of scrub*

☐ *binoculars (nice to have)*

☐ *a comfortable backpack to put it all in*

☐ *a good hat, and, of course...*

☐ *a good horse! (Though most of you will have to rely on your own two legs).*

If you really aren't sure what you need, you could pack the stuff I've suggested, then go out in the woods somewhere, park your car, go three hundred yards up a trail, and pretend you broke your ankle and are going to have to spend the night. Over the course of that night, you'll quickly figure out the happy medium between carrying too much and not having enough. Hunters are usually better prepared with layers, rations, and a good knife (at a bare minimum); similarly, hikers at least have some extra clothes to layer on and off, and some snacks and water; but mountain bikers often don't have extra clothes and all they have is a water bottle and sometimes a bike repair kit (which won't help them comfortably survive overnight).

Child Survival programs have a very small survival kit that they recommend, and this is also good to consider, because most of us have this stuff in our houses right now. Colleen Politano's book *Lost in the Woods: Child Survival for Parents and Teachers* recommends:

☐ *a heavy-duty Ziploc sandwich bag (to put everything in but also to use as a container for collecting and drinking water from)*

☐ *a high-energy snack (trail mix in its own Ziploc bag)*

☐ *a whistle to call for help (three short blasts)*

☐ *a signalling device (small piece of cardboard wrapped in aluminum foil or pocket mirror)*

☐ *a large, bright orange garbage bag with a slit pre-cut for the face opening*

People always ask me what is in my saddle bags on the show, and most of it you've just read. I also carry my slicker behind the saddle. I have gloves if it gets cold, but having said that, if it's raining, you're better off without gloves (unless they're waterproof), as gloves just keep the cold against your hands.

I mentioned that I don't use sunglasses for tracking, and I should explain why. If you're searching or looking, sure, use sunglasses to protect your eyes, but if you're tracking, sunglasses can make it harder or impossible to see some tracks. I taught tracking to a group of women at an outdoors conference. I was pointing out sign here and there, and one of the women said she couldn't see a track that was pretty much on the end of her nose. She was getting frustrated and took off her sunglasses to rub the bridge of her nose. When she did, she looked down again and there was the track – she could see it no problem. I looked through her sunglasses and, sure as heck, I couldn't see it either. Sometimes, tracking is trial and error. (Luckily, in reading this you get some of the wisdom I had to learn by making errors).

If you forget some of your supplies at home, there are some "home remedies" in the bush. But like some mushrooms are delicious and others are poisonous, make sure you're totally certain that you have the right item before you add insult (or poisoning) to injury.

The next list is specifically for items you typically take with you if you're tracking (in addition to what's above):

- ☐ *tracking stick – ski pole, broom handle, walking stick, or tree branch*
- ☐ *different colour elastics (to use for width and length measurements of the track and step)*
- ☐ *digital camera (take a photo of the map, tread pattern in a track)*
- ☐ *flagging tape (to mark a trail)*
- ☐ *tape measure*
- ☐ *track identification form (template helps with drawing a track and communicating information about it)*

For SAR, I'd also bring plastic bags, a permanent marker, latex gloves, and tweezers (for handling evidence), my bright yellow jacket identifying that I was part of the SAR team; and I'd have my gear bag with a bunch of stuff for searching or tracking across different terrains, like:

- *rubber boots*
- *hip waders*
- *helmet or hard-hat*
- *rope gear, and*
- *life jacket.*

Of course, if you're going to be outdoors tracking, knowing some basic survival and outdoors skills wouldn't hurt. You wouldn't want to make the mistake of crawling prone in a patch of poison ivy to blend in with your surroundings. That would make tracking really miserable.

Part of your surroundings

To find something that or someone who may not want to be found, you need to be part of your surroundings. This means being quiet, and being invisible. This applies to the military, hunters, and the hunted, including those aspiring to be on the Mantracker series themselves one day. This does not apply to SAR as you're not trying to sneak up on a lost child, or be difficult to see by other **Hasty Teams**.

If you're making too much noise, you may not hear your prey's noise, and equally bad, they may hear you coming. There are times you can use noise to your advantage to flush out the prey towards someone else, but generally, you don't want to spook your prey. Choosing the proper clothing that doesn't make a lot of noise is as important for trackers as it is for human prey. Don't wear nylon or corduroy that makes a lot of noise when you walk unless you want to be heard. Before you buy any new outdoor gear, while you're in the store, sweep your hand up and down the sleeves, legs, front and back of the camo clothes you're thinking of buying. If they're not quiet, don't buy it. The sound of a zipper or Velcro opening can travel a long ways in the woods, as can the ring of a cell phone. Avoid smacking your gum, whistling or humming, cracking your knuckles, etc. You may be so used to making these noises that you think you're being perfectly stealthy.

I've tracked people so unaware of the noise they were making, even when they weren't talking, that all I could think was: "These boys couldn't sneak up on a rock concert!"

Quiet movement is not only about clothing, but also about how you move. Learn to look where you're stepping to avoid snapping twigs. Walk softly: don't drag or shuffle your feet. Or, just ride a horse. Overall, you need to be aware of the noises you're making, with your body, clothing, and movements.

I've said it before and I'll say it again, people think that the woods are so quiet, but they're actually quite noisy. The noises are just different. Instead of honking horns, you have bird calls; instead of angry drivers yelling, you have chipmunks cussing you out for getting too close to their nest. If you do make a noise, and think you're about to be spotted, freeze for ten seconds and keep your silhouette as small and invisible as possible.

Being invisible is easier when you wear camouflage suiting your environment (forest, desert, or snow colours, depending on where you are and what season it is). You can also camouflage your face with paint (or charcoal). Ever wonder why hunters wear plaid? It's harder for animals to spot. Surely you've seen military helmets with branches on them? It breaks up the silhouette of a round human head.

Avoid reflecting light by not wearing shiny belt buckles, or flashing your pearly whites too often. Remember if you're wearing a backpack, your body may be hidden, but your backpack may peek out and reveal your hiding place.

Also, avoid leaving your own sign, and that includes your garbage. Don't be stupid and lazy. Nature is not your dumping ground. I just can't understand how some people out there think the outdoors is for getting rid of their garbage. Respect the land! If you pack it in, pack it out.

Aside from the forest fire risk, cigarette butts are garbage. If you smoke, bring a tin with you to pack out your butts.

You're also not part of your surroundings if you smell different from everything around you. I've never seen beautiful women come charging through the bush to find the outdoorsman covered in men's body spray, but bugs sure are attracted to it, so don't bathe in perfume or cologne in the morning. Speaking of bathing, if you haven't bathed in a week (or don't know what antiperspirant is), or you're a heavy smoker, your smell can also make you stand out like a lump in the middle of your forehead.

Practice

While paying attention and problem-solving, and being physically fit, patient, present, persistent, positive, prepared and part of your surroundings are all important and can help you become a better tracker, it's all for nothing if you don't practice your skills. You won't get to be a good carpenter just by reading a book on carpentry. You won't be a good tracker if don't go out and try it for yourself. Get out there and look for some sign, see what story it can tell you.

Chapter 9:
Interpreting sign: by category

"Common Sense is that which judges the things given to it by other senses."

Leonardo da Vinci

"Interpretation is 90%."

Terry Grant

Let's review a few things about sign that have been covered so far. Sign is left by humans or animals as they pass through an area; and it can be detected by sight, hearing, touch, or smell. Sign can be categorized by where it is found (top sign or ground sign); and whether it is your prey's (conclusive sign) or corroborates your prey's trail of sign (corroborating sign). It can also be categorized by the type of sign left behind, and this is the way I best like to talk about it. So, here's some more detail about the classifications of sign introduced earlier: impressions, transfers, damage, disturbances, and things left behind.

Impressions

Some people might prefer that I call this *compressions* as opposed to *impressions*, but it's my book, so I get to choose what I call them!

Tracks are the impressions that we look for the most. Tread patterns are not unique, but are distinctive, and they're the most conclusive sign, short of someone dropping something.

- *Typically, in the same ground conditions, the deeper the track, the heavier the person (and/or the load they're carrying).*

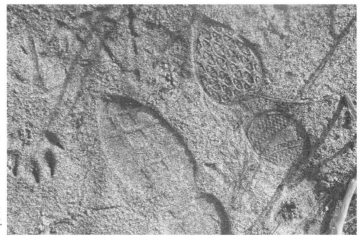

The person on the left was heavier (or the load they were carrying was heavier) than the person on the right. The track is deeper.

A momma moose's tracks are deeper and more defined than her calf's.

- *Sometimes you'll notice round marks every two or so steps, and that might be a sign of someone using a walking stick. The stick doesn't distribute weight as much as the sole of a shoe, so even in harder ground, walking stick marks are often visible, even when boot prints aren't showing up at all.*
- *You may find signs of a place where people rested or camped. The grass or dirt may be compressed from someone having sat or slept there.*

Someone left a bum-impression here from sitting.

- *In the fall or spring, you'll also see impressions in the leaves. It's not conclusive sign, but if you find them in a patch of leaves with a partial print at either end of it, then those impressions in the leaves are corroborating sign.*

Transfers

You're looking for transfer anytime the landscape changes.

> • *If you tromp on ground through the forest and then cross a stream, dirt may transfer into the water, and water may transfer onto the earth or rocks on the other side of the stream. If you've been in water and come out dripping, you're going to leave water drops on logs, rocks, and vegetation for a while. Depending on how wet you got or how deep the water, your trail of residual water will change.*

Note the faint water transfer on the rocks.

- *Going from grass onto a porch, you can bring grass onto the wood or stain the wood with the green chlorophyll of the grass transferred from the bottom of your footwear.*

- *If you stepped in sand or sawdust and then on leaves, you'd track sand or sawdust onto the leaves.*

Pine needles were transferred forward into the mud and crushed into the track.

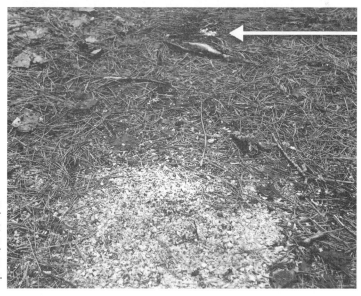

Aside from the obvious transfer right in front of the pile, the sawdust transfer carried forward for several yards.

- Mud could also be transferred to a log as you step out of a little mud puddle up onto the log (or over it). If it's a shallow mud puddle, a gob of mud might be missing (disturbance), and carried forward with you. There, the lack of something tells the tracker something, even if they don't find the transfer.

- Blood can be left on barbed wire by people who chose to jump a fence. Injured people or animals can leave blood drops or smears pretty much anywhere. I've been asked before to track animals that hunters have wounded and not killed. If you know an animal has been hit reasonably hard, don't start tracking it right away: give it time to die in peace on its own. If it's a bad shot, you have to track the animal until you can dispatch of it humanely. In that case, you'll usually be following blood drops on the ground and blood smears on trees in addition to tracks.

Damage

While you may notice raspberries missing from a bush that a hiker ate on the way by, a lot of the natural damage that you'll see is from the animals, where they nibbled branches, scratched bark or rubbed it away. Humans are a bit more like bulls in china shops when it comes to natural disturbances and damage. Whether it's a flower that's two or three inches high or fireweed two or three feet high, deer can walk through and not crush one plant. Humans will hit two or three of them and the plants will be bent down or broken in the direction of travel. Perhaps one exception is that both man and animal will tear through cobwebs, leaving the same damage (only perhaps at different heights).

Relating to damage, here's some behaviour you wouldn't see from an animal:

- *Some people snap twigs off trees as they go in the bush, to not get lost, or out of habit, and I'm one of them. When I walk through the bush, I snap off dead twigs and break them into smaller pieces, to show where I've been. Following a path of broken twigs can be as conclusive as boot prints, if breaking twigs is your prey's habit.*
- *Charred earth or sticks (though you might classify the remnants of a campfire as something left behind, too, if your prey packed in their own firewood). Regardless, you might be able to age the fire pit by poking into the ashes with a stick to see if there are any embers left. You can also hold your hand over the area to feel for warmth. Then you can "sweep" around the camp to find tracks showing a direction of travel. You can start at the fire and walk out in a spiral, looking for tracks.*

Here there is damage of the campfire and a cereal box left behind by humans, and damage to the box from an animal.

- *If you find that a small tree was cut down and only the stump remains, perhaps the prey was making a walking stick, or dragging it behind them to erase their tracks. Start looking for impressions from a stick, or a lack of sign.*

What made this damage? At first glance you might think was from an animal, because it looks chewed, but with a closer look, and no teeth marks in the exposed wood, and based on the location, it was clear that the bark was damaged by a dirt bike.

Disturbances

Disturbances are where something has been moved but not broken (that would be damage). So the example of more damage being caused by humans than deer in fireweed is useful to think of here too. Deer (actually, most animals with hooves) tend to lift their feet almost straight up and then put them straight down. Humans churn up the earth more – we're clumsier, and have bigger feet.

The most common is a **negative imprint**. This is when an indentation is left where a rock or stick used to be and that has since been kicked, moved, stepped on and pushed, or tripped over. If someone stepped on the side of a rock or branch already partially in the earth, there would be a negative void on one side of the rock or branch and fresh dirt on the other side.

Vegetation disturbances are probably the next most common. This happens when the ground is covered in pine needles or fallen leaves. You won't see tracks. You'll have to look for disturbances – where something (like leaves, needles, cones) is missing or is piled up in an area. Another example is grass paths where the grass is bent over and hasn't sprung back up yet. Same goes for fireweed, lying there like a dead seagull, pointing out the direction of travel. When people are trying to evade me, I've seen them leave a road or path, so as not to leave tracks; but the dark path they leave in the leaves, from crushing and disturbing them, is just as easy to follow.

I'm pointing at the spot where the prey decided to leave the road and move to the leaves. You can see impressions in the form of tracks leading up to me, and disturbances in the leaves continuing away from me.

Negative imprints and vegetation disturbances are quite common, but there are some more non-standard disturbances, including some relating to our other senses that we can look at, too:

- Silt disturbed from the bottom of a puddle (see the photo on page 95 (bottom), in the next section on "Tracking in different conditions: Puddles"); or dew knocked off leaves.
- If prey was climbing up a steep hill, you'll find rocks disturbed or dirt with a depression from just the ball of the foot. If the prey was going downhill, you'll see longer slide or skid marks as a disturbance in the steep hill and deeper heel strike. It's nothing definite, but it's definitely human.

If you want to figure out the direction of travel in this sand dune, the defined heel strike and the slide mark should tell you that they're going downhill.

- *You can also watch the behaviour of wildlife – they'll run or move if prey invades their territory. I've watched deer before to figure out the prey's movement. I knew that something had chased that whitetail out of the coulee: it ran away from the prey, stopped and looked back, showing me where my little rabbits were likely hiding.*
- *In the same vein, smelling smoke from a campfire or hearing the snap of branches that someone stepped on are disturbances (to the scent or the quiet or the air).*

Things left behind

Aside from the things animals leave behind such as fur, feathers, scat, pellets, and urine (that we'll talk about more in "Tracking Animals"), humans add a whole new element of "litter," whether it's on purpose or not.

- *I've seen clothing left as conclusive proof, like wet socks at the side of a stream. Ten to fifteen percent of people with hypothermia start to peel off their clothing.*

A discarded, or forgotten coat on the ground

- *There are five levels where things can be left behind: at the feet, knees, hips, shoulder/head, and above the head (if something is thrown or falls from a height). This makes sense based on the parts of our bodies that are widest, or what we protect first. People tend to worry about their shoulders and head. So there will be some damage, and often bits of clothing or thread on trees at that level. If the vegetation is really thick, people bend over, keeping everything away from their face, so you'll find sign at hip level, too. For animals, their fur gets caught on branches as sign left behind too, and the height of the sign depends on the size of the animal.*

- *Cigarette butts, gum and granola bar wrappers, and drink containers are unfortunately common sign in the bush. City slickers figure if they're going into the woods they have to survive on granola bars and trail mix. People eating on the move always drop some of what they're eating, and that can give you a clue as to how long ago they were there. Smarties and chocolate chips will be left longer by the birds or chipmunks; they'll clean up the raisins and nuts and leave the Smarties. If you only find Smarties, you'll know that the eater is farther ahead of you; if there are still peanuts and raisins there, they can't be too far ahead.*

Things left behind: The squirrels haven't grabbed the peanuts and sunflower seeds, so this spilled trail mix is less than a day old. Sadly, the shell casings, diaper, beer can. and cell phone were found within a mile of each other in otherwise pristine bush.

Another way of looking at tracking is not by the category, but by the conditions you might find yourself in, so this next section goes through tracking in different conditions.

Chapter 10:
Tracking in different conditions

"On some ground, the only way you'll find a track is if someone is standing in it."

Terry Grant

"You're at the mercy of Mother Nature...and she always wins."

Terry Grant

Tracking is a completely different game when you're tracking on different terrains, and in different weather conditions. I'll start with different terrains and we'll move on from there. I'll also answer the question of my favourite and least favourite places to track.

Along a road/path

- *On a roadway, look for shine. Even if you can't see it right where you are, look farther down the road, change your perspective, and look behind you.*
- *Once you find tracks leading onto a road, if there are no prints, and no shine on the road, scan in a wide zigzag pattern and concentrate on the four-foot band on either side of the road for exit points.*

- *Someone moving down the side of the road or path may not leave toe kicks or boot prints, but may transfer mud onto a leaf, or may leave a negative imprint from dislodging a rock or stick from its resting place. The boot print would be the conclusive sign, and the other two would be corroborating sign. You may want to continue on the road and watch for tracks later leaving the bush and rejoining the road if you follow the tracks off the road and lose the trail.*
- *When someone is running, their steps are farther apart and there is more disturbance on the ground, including longer toe kicks (the push-off of each step flicks more dirt farther back).*
- *Fresh dirt toe kicks have darker dirt in them, as the unearthed darker dirt hasn't dried out yet. Also, if the dirt in the toe kick is still loose and can be easily brushed away, it's fresh.*

In the bush

In thick bush, you're looking less for ground sign and more for top sign like snapped twigs, missing leaves, bark off trees, or a hand print left from jumping off of a log. Less subtle sign that you may see in dense bush includes threads left hanging on a tree, or carabiners with compasses that were hanging on a backpack and that snagged on a tree. I've also found hats, binoculars, lighters, fire starter, and a whole heap of litter (gum wrappers, drink containers, cigarette butts), among other things.

Another issue that comes up with dense bush tracking is that you may not notice the clouds coming in, it may just seem overcast. In Northern Ontario, the canopy is so thick, it starts to rain before you realize it might rain.

The trick to tracking in the bush is to think like the prey and look around at where you might go, or how you might travel, then look for sign in those areas:

- *Especially in dense bush, look for game trails that might make travelling easier. Sometimes you can even see the hole prey left in the bush.*

- *Near a log or fence, watch for flattened areas where they have hopped over. Fences with barbs might also have bits of clothing, fur, or blood on them. Look on the top of logs for scuff or scrape marks or transfers.*
- *If tracks are going into an area of bush, check around the outside for exit tracks. If there aren't any, you know they're probably hiding in the area.*
- *Cobwebs can help you eliminate a direction of travel: if there is a big one at chest height, then unless your prey is hours ahead of you, they didn't go that way.*

Through vegetation

- *Under the "Direction and speed of travel" and "Disturbances" and "Damage" there were different vegetation examples given. Vegetation points to your direction of travel. Also, humans make more disturbance than animals, mainly because of the size of their feet and laziness of movement lifting them.*

Here's a human foot impression left in moss

- *In grass of most any length, a silver path through the grass means your prey walked away from where you're standing. A dark path through the grass means they came towards you. I think this happens from the way the light hits the grass. If you're looking for an easy way to remember which colour is which direction, think of the Lone Ranger and what he said every time he jumped on his horse, Silver (if you've never seen him in action, you can always check it out on YouTube). He said: "Hi-ho, Silver! Away!" (If you're a real fan, you'll know he actually said "hi-yo", but we won't split blades of grass here.) So how does that help? If you see a silver trail in the grass, they were walking away from you. I have to laugh when people walk backwards in grass, because it doesn't change the clues for directionality, and I know it just slowed them down.*

Here I see three silver paths going towards the mountains (Oh and here is the answer from page 54)

- *Grass pushed down into a track that hasn't had time to spring back means it's probably less than half an hour old.*
- *In pine needles or fallen leaves there are no tracks, you have to look for disturbances.*
- *When a plant is stepped on and crushed against a rock or the earth, if the plant is still green and not wilting or browning/yellowing when you find it, your prey is likely less than an hour ahead of you. Bruising may not always be readily apparent: often you have to look at the underside of the leaves, because some thicker vegetation that has been stepped on bruises on the bottom side only. See page 49, "Aging: Time of travel" for other photos.*

This leaf was stepped on several hours ago since the damage on the leaf has yellowed through to the front of the leaf and is dry.

- *On a steep hillside, I've seen fireweed knocked down and little dirt piles beside the plant, showing the prey went straight up that steep incline.*
- *Young maple saplings pushed out of the way at hip level just whip back again, filling the void, but you might find leaves broken off or partially broken leaves.*

Dew

One time on a dewy morning, I couldn't find any sign in a field of low vegetation. I thought I was hooped, but then I worked on the theory that sometimes the absence of sign is sign. I looked closer and found a path where the dew had been knocked off the leaves and grass, showing me that someone or something had passed through there. Along the way, I also found a vegetation disturbance where the bottom side of some ground leaves were facing up, having been turned and bent when stepped on. Sure, there may have been no tracks, but there was a bucket-load of sign. You can also look for the absence of dew on the leaves of low tree branches or on bushes, where the water droplets were knocked off as prey brushed past them.

Dew missing from vegetation can point to a direction of travel

Harder ground and rock

On harder earth, the imprint is less deep. The lighter the prey and any load they are carrying, the less deep the imprint. Where a 130-pound woman barely leaves a track, a 200-pound man's track is quite visible in the same terrain.

In colder environments, like September in the Yukon, it's harder to find tracks and establish a direction of travel. The cold ground is harder, near frozen, and not really impressionable. But working to your advantage is that, in the fall, the trees have fewer leaves providing cover for the prey to hide in.

If prey gets onto rock and stays on it, it's tough to track. These are the types of conditions where I'm known to say things like: "You couldn't track a bulldozer in this crap!"

You can only really work on the transitions getting on or off the rock. You look for mud/dirt transfer getting onto the rock, and look for tracks getting off, too. On the rock itself, you can only look for disturbed moss, or negative impressions from small pebbles being kicked out of place, or white scratch marks where a pebble or stone was dragged across the rock's surface or a walking stick with a metal tip scarred the rock. Other than that, you might find a red or green colour rubbed onto the rock from a vine or leaf that's been stepped on.

You can see that someone transferred the green from the leaf to the rock, but other than that there is no sign that they've been on the rock. The front side of the leaf shows no damage immediately.

Mud

Soft mud oozes back into the track, like sand (check out the ooze below in the top of the track on the left). You get an impression, but not the conclusive sign of a track. In very wet muddy terrain, if you find a footprint and the water hasn't oozed back into the track yet, it's very fresh. In the right type of mud or clay, you can get a near perfect impression, indicating time lines. Mud track sides are sharp and square when fresh (the partial track in the photo on the right is well defined, so very fresh). As they age, the edges fall in.

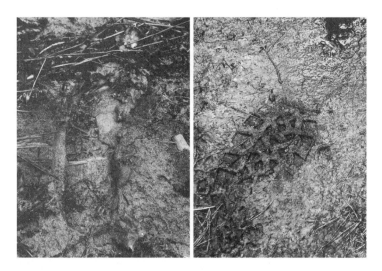

Mud is often like the icing on a cake that is left out overnight; if you stick your finger in the icing to taste it, it cracks, but is still mush underneath. Now, I won't be sticking my finger in mud for a snack, but I think the point is made here: sunshine and wind give mud a crust.

After or during a light rain, as someone or something walks through the mud, the toe kick uncovers the dry dirt underneath. Their "foot" grabs the top crust of earth and peels it away, leaving a lighter, sandier layer exposed beneath. Ground that gets stuck to their "foot" also gets transferred forwards, too. The lighter tracks or partial tracks are easy to spot, and the transfer is an added bonus, both making it easier to track. It's often easier to age the transfer of mud than the actual track, because you don't have to step in the mud and see how long it takes to ooze back or fill up with water. Instead you get a quick feel for how dry the transfer is.

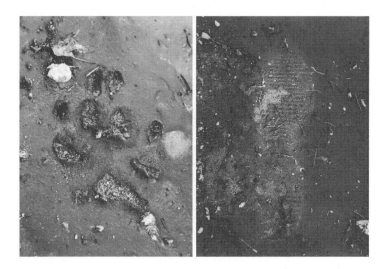

Also, people who've stepped in mud will usually stomp their feet at some point to get it off of their boots. Even if you can't find any tracks immediately, look within ten feet for a stomp that is defined by a lot of mud transfer. It's definite proof that the person who went through the mud went in the direction you're following.

Puddles

I like puddles. People don't like to get their feet wet, so they usually skirt around them or jump over them, so I know exactly where to look for sign. Also, the ground around the puddle is usually softer and better for seeing impressions. When someone jumps over a puddle, the jump leads to better tracks before and after the puddle. The jumping-off leg leaves a big toe kick, and the landing foot's impression is much deeper than normal.

In fact, large puddles that almost span the whole trail often present a **track trap** – a natural or man-made area where, if someone passes through it, they are bound to leave sign. In the photo that follows, with thick bush on both sides, this is a track trap because it forces someone to either edge of the puddle.

Children will walk straight through puddles (and usually stomp in them a couple of times, too). Adults, much more concerned about dry feet and less concerned with fun, will walk through them if wearing waterproof footwear, or if they are trying to be evasive, thinking that there will be no sign left. They're wrong: silt is moved from the bottom of a puddle from someone stepping through it. The silt is disturbed from where it was and settles outside where the footprint was, usually leaving a trail of lighter patches slightly larger than the original footprint.

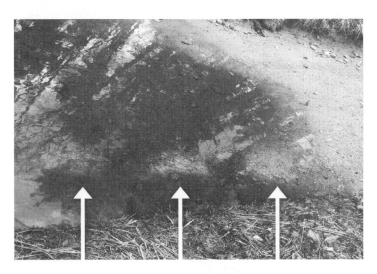

When there is a perfect carpet of leaves at the bottom of a puddle, there is no silt to disturb, but the dirt from someone's footwear will be transferred on top of the leaves. Also, when you leave any puddle, you kick water forwards with you, transferring water to the next area. Depending how dry the ground is (and how close you are), you may still see the water transfer.

Sometimes you see mud still swirling in a mud puddle, and that usually means someone or something just stepped it in minutes ago. The faster the swirl is moving, the closer you are to finding them. I get a rush when I see the mud swirl if it's along a path of conclusive evidence – it's a real adrenaline buzz to know you're that close.

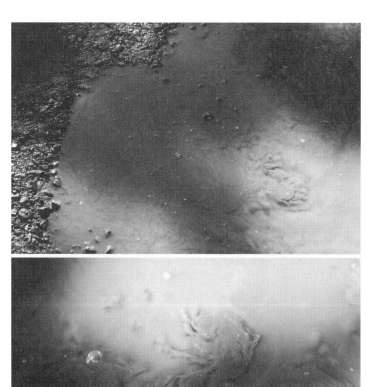

Near water

In addition to what was just said about tracking near or through puddles, there are other water tracking situations to think about as well including creeks, rivers, and shorelines of lakes.

- *For puddles, creeks, and rivers, you look for: deep impressions where someone might have jumped from or to; water or mud transfer on rocks sticking out of the water or on either shore. The transfer on the shore can show you the direction of travel.*

There's no transfer on the rocks, but there is a partial print from where someone jumped from (or to).

- *On the edge of a lake or large river, people will sometimes walk right along the water's edge assuming that the water will wash away their tracks. I once tracked a couple who didn't walk close enough to have the water wash away the tracks. It made for real easy tracking. It was such a boneheaded mistake, but they probably didn't want to get their feet wet; running in wet boots is no fun. In each of the photos below, all of the tracks were erased, but one, and that's all I need to get the conclusive sign I need.*

- In a slow-moving river or creek, just like in puddles, there is a fine layer of silt at the bottom of the bed, and so you can see every step from the lighter patches left exposed by the disturbed silt. You may also get a butt impression or scuff marks where someone sat down to take off their boots to cross the water and foot prints going in. Also, you get the water transfer on the way out.
- In fast-moving water, there is no silt to be disturbed, and you can't see into the water. All you can do is hope for entrance or exit tracks or sign like transfer. Once you have a point of entry, your job is finding the exit point. Look at the river and judge what you'd do if you were in it. Are there rapids up ahead that you'd want to avoid? Is the water getting crotch deep so that you'd prefer to get out? Typically, where I'd leave the water, they prey has, too, and I usually find sign.
- In wet clay or mud near water, after it is stepped in, the sides ooze back in, so the track is smaller than what you'd expect. Don't get fooled into thinking that it's not your prey's. In really mushy clay or mud, the track is gone, because the clay folds back in, but there will still be the shape of a foot in the mud. You might come across a perfect foot-shaped puddle, or the outline of a boot print with no definition or pattern.

- If someone is trying to evade you, they can be a bit predictable at creeks and small rivers: they cross it to make you think they have continued in that direction, but nine times out of ten, if you see a couple prints following the creek on the other side, they are going to cross back to the side they started from.

Sand

If you walk down a beach barefoot, you get a real clear understanding of how tracks look in differing types of terrain.

- *In packed sand right by the water's edge, you might leave almost no track at all. Someone 100 pounds heavier might leave a slight track.*
- *Moving inshore, the sand gets softer, and you can leave perfect bare footprints with every toe delineated.*
- *Farthest away from the water, where the sand is dry and loose, you leave a footprint, but no detail. The print is shaped such that you know it's human, but the lack of definition makes it hard to know if it was a 12-year-old girl or a 50-year-old man who made the depression in the sand. You have to make your own step in the sand and compare the impression you've made with the track you've found to estimate foot size and or weight, compared to your own.*

It's really hard to tell who left what tracks in loose dry sand!

- *Overall, tracks in sand are deeper and less defined. Toe kicks are usually more evident, leaving a divot with sand pushed up behind it. Heel strikes are also more evident, again assuming you're in soft, but not dry, sand.*
- *You can determine the speed of someone's travel by the length of the step and stride on the beach. You can test yourself and see which set of tracks were made by someone walking versus someone jogging or running, as the faster they were moving, the farther apart the tracks would be spaced (and yes, the length of the person's legs factors into this, too).*

The more spaced out deeper tracks mean that someone was running or jogging

- *When I was tracking in the desert once, staring right at the sand around me, I couldn't see tracks. By blurring my vision a bit and looking just above the sand 50 feet away, my lower peripheral vision caught sight of the lines of tracks (but I had to stay focused, or like with shine, if I looked away, I'd lose sight of them).*

- *Here's something I noticed recently when I was trying out tracks on the beach one day. If you walk forwards in damp sand your toe kick usually removes the sand that would otherwise have been left between your toes. Walking backwards, because you lift your feet straight up more so than walking forwards, the ridges of sand from between your toes are still there. You can still see that the step and stride is shorter and the pitch is off more with walking backwards, but there is this extra indication from sand if people are barefoot when you're tracking them.*

Note the full toe marks, shorter step and more pitch in the tracks on the left - showing backwards walking.

- *In soft sand, where your foot sinks-in an inch or more, you'll see sand dragged forward from the track (like in snow or mud).*

Swamp

What can I say about tracking through swamp other than avoid doing it. I don't track through a bog. I treat it like a puddle and track around it, looking for entry and exit points. Luckily, most people (and most horses) won't tramp through a swamp if there is another option. Not only is it very hard to travel through because of the differing viscosities of the conditions, but it's also very, very unpredictable. One second you can be only a couple inches deep, then before you know it you're waist deep in muck. The only good thing about that is that the same holds for the person you're tracking. If you stick to looking for entry or exit points, you will see mud, muck, or slime transfer onto the ground at the exit point.

Lighting

I already talked about the need to get a new perspective to view tracks, based on the lighting and the amount of contrast in them. The amount of light and the position of the sun can dramatically affect how easy it is to see tracks:

- *High noon makes it harder to track. When the sun gets up that high, no shadows are cast across the track, so you can't see the depth. Standing right over it, you'd see nothing. You either have to shade it, or try and look at it from a different angle. Notice how much better you can see the barefoot print in the second photo once it's been shaded.*

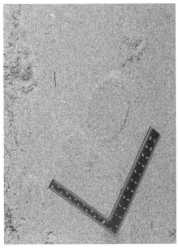

- *The reverse can also be true, that you can't see tracks in shade. But with morning sun, the shadows pop, and all of a sudden you've got a direction of travel to follow.*
- *Anytime you're having a hard time making out a track, and are trying to see if it is the right track to follow, you can use a piece of white Bristol board or your hat or body to block the light and then use a mirror or a good strong flashlight to reflect light across the track. Sometimes at high noon, just putting yourself between the sun and the track and casting your shadow across the track will make it pop. In heavily shaded or dark areas, some people wear headlamps on their shins to help them see tracks.*

- *Night tracking is tough to do, but it is possible under perfect conditions. If your prey is walking down a road, you may be able to see their tracks with a flashlight. Tracking in the bush at night is close to futile without the proper lighting. You might track 50 yards all night. But if you waited until morning, you could track the same distance in a minute and a half. Also, most people won't travel at night, as they can't see any better than you can. The big exception is in SAR if you are on a lost soul's trail your search manager might have the search continue through the night.*

Rain

Rain can really help with tracking. It keeps the ground soft, people's steps expose the light earth underneath, and puddles act as track traps. A nice steady rain is good to track in (assuming you're dressed for it) because it gives you a good timeline. If you know it started raining at 11am, then when you find a track filled with water at noon, you know that track has been there longer than the bright partial track beside it, where only the top crust of the earth has been lifted and hasn't filled with any water.

- *Softer earth means that prints are more visible as the foot sinks into the ground more.*
- *When the earth gets so soft that it turns into mud, you get more transfer to track.*
- *With a lot of rain, you can age how long ago the prey passed by through looking at how much water is in the track. You can make your own track beside it for comparison, too, to see how long it takes to fill your track. Also rain on an old track diffuses everything: it mellows everything out to the same state.*
- *Leaves would be crushed into a track if they fell during the rain and someone walked through after that. But if leaves are just lying on top, covering part of a track, and not pressed into it, it's a clear indication that tracks were being made before the rain/wind.*
- *Wet leaves will be pushed up at the back of each footprint instead of a dirt toe kick, especially if the prey is travelling uphill, as their feet would be sliding.*

Snow

Although it sucks to be in it, snow is easy to track in, unless you're tracking someone and then the snow hits and hides all the tracks. Sometimes, when conditions are relatively constant, it can be as easy as following an obvious trail. On a SAR mission once in the winter, a teen had gone hunting and hadn't returned. We went to his last-known point and, after three days, we picked up a trail about three days old. Sadly, we followed those tracks right to where he had fallen asleep and never woke up.

While it's near impossible to not leave tracks in snow, and you can usually get a good indication of the direction and speed of travel, it can be really hard to age a track in snow.

- *Not unlike sand, there are many different kinds of snow. Good snowball-making snow will hold a track print beautifully; other kinds of snow are more granular just fill a track and leave only a depression (just like sand).*
- *If it stayed one constant temperature, you could probably age a track to within an hour, but that doesn't happen a lot in the winter. In firm mud, you might be able to see a track that looks brand new, even though it was made four to five hours ago, if there was no wind or direct sun. But in snow, a track can be frozen perfectly for days when it isn't exposed to the elements.*
- *Again as with mud, aging the track in snow is sometimes easier done by aging the toe kick or snow dragged forwards. If the snow sprayed out is still loose and not stuck to the snow below it, it is fresher. Once that sprayed snow is exposed to a bit of sun, melts, then freezes slightly to the snow below it, it's been there longer. I usually use my hand and see if I can move the snow spray easily, like moving sand on a table, to know if it is fresh. If it's stuck and you can't easily separate the two layers, it's been there longer.*
- *The area of disturbance of a track gets bigger with a hard crust; the foot breaks through the crust and often pulls in part of the surrounding crust, too.*

Tracks in the shade or in protected areas last much longer

- *If there is less than an inch of snow, you'll still get a toe kick in the snow. As soon as you get much more than that, the snow will be sprayed in the direction of travel, since you drag the snow with you in the direction you're going as you lift your foot up through it.*
- *Sometimes, you'll see what looks like tracks of someone dragging their feet, but really they just aren't lifting their feet clear of the snow. It may not actually be an indication of them carrying a heavy load or being tired or injured. I was surprised just how much drag was left from walking normally in more than one inch of snow.*

- *Wind helps preserve a track in certain types of snow. Loose snow drifts, and the drift snow is harder than fallen snow.*
- *With the first or last snows of a season, where they melt away pretty fast, compressed snow like a snowmobile trail will stay the longest before it melts away. Same goes for tracks, if there is enough snow to compress, and if drifted snow got added to the track.*

Wind

Wind is less a condition for tracking in and of itself than a factor that affects the other conditions. Most of all, wind affects the aging of tracks. Tracks exposed to wind dry out and the edges crumble quicker, so that a track four hours old might look much older. Also, wind blows stuff onto tracks – like leaves and pine needles. I once found a bear track with pine needles in the track about 25 feet from a pine tree. There hadn't been any wind to speak of for three days, so I was pretty confident that the track was at least three days old, and I didn't need to worry much about camping in that spot.

Auditory and scent tracking can also be affected by the wind. A light breeze can carry a human voice quite a distance, especially if you're in a valley, and it sounds like the people are right beside you. Scents can also be carried farther by the wind, but also dissipate faster.

Weather and seasons

Wind, rain, sun, snow, heat, and sleet all affect tracks and tracking. As a tracker, you need to retain information about what the weather's been doing for the last few days, and have an understanding of how that might affect tracks or other sign. You also have to remember that the weather in town is often completely different than the weather in the foothills of the mountains, or on the edge of the Great Lakes, etc. You've heard of lake effect? When you're brought into a SAR mission, it wouldn't be too bright to assume that, because you had no snow that night where you live, where you'll be searching automatically didn't get snow either.

- *A track in shade or sun will age totally differently.*
- *Sun dries out mud tracks faster, evaporates water transfer faster, melts snow faster, etc. In your driveway, after a light snow, make a bunch of tracks and watch how long they stay around based on whether they were in the sun or shade (see the photo of this on page 51 under "Prove it!").*
- *Wind, rain, and snow affect tracks the most (that's why they got their own sections before this): not only do they mess with aging a track, both can obliterate tracks or cover them up.*

Spring

- *Spring is the easiest time to track because the ground is soft, and tender new grass and vegetation are easily bruised. The trees haven't filled out with leaves, so prey have less cover to hide in. Working against you, though, is that the weather is still unpredictable, and you might experience snow, rain, frost at nights, and wild temperature variations.*

Summer

- *In summer, the ground is slightly harder, but the longer grasses give better evidence of people travelling through the area. The weather is also the most consistent. The downfall is probably the bugs. While they don't affect tracks, the little button-heads buzzing around your head can really affect your concentration. The other downfall is that with the heat, wind, and/or direct sunlight, water transfer on rocks dries out more quickly, giving you less time to find that kind of sign before it disappears.*

Fall

- *Fall is harder, literally and figuratively. The ground itself is harder, and leaves already on the ground don't bruise. There is more ground cover, because of fallen leaves, making it harder to see tracks, but there is usually more disturbance to follow. Same as in the spring, the leaves off the trees provide less cover to mask prey's movements.*
- *Tracks that froze at night would take longer to deteriorate and appear a lot more recent than they are, so a tracker would need to know that there had been a frost and take that into account. There might still be frost in the track, if it was made earlier.*
- *If a track is made in the fall at the right time just before the ground freezes, it could be there all winter, looking pretty much the same (if it's sheltered from the snow).*

Winter

- *Winter tracking is the most specialized, so it got a whole section for tracking in the snow. The downside is that it's miserable tracking because it's so damn cold.*

Urban tracking

It's a location rather than a condition, but people ask if I do any urban tracking, so I'll gloss over it for you here. Urban tracking is a whole different ball of wax that I've got almost nothing to do with. Really, it shouldn't be called tracking at all, because it is searching. You can't track on cement or asphalt, other than noticing some transfer onto it or exit marks. You aren't really tracking people if you're looking for them in the city: you're just working off their routine and usual haunts to try and find them. You go on visual sightings and leads, just like when the police are tracking down suspects. The only way I can see to calling it tracking is if you have dogs involved in the search, because they are following sign – they are scent tracking.

There are teams of urban trackers who are often called in after natural disasters to find people and bodies, but it's a specialized form of searching. In Pine Lake, Alberta, I participated in an urban search after a tornado. You look for people under houses, trees, and debris. They're looking to be found, so unlike with tracking, you listen for sounds more. Searchers have to have good hearing to hear someone tapping or calling from under debris.

Urban searches also take place for missing children and the elderly (with dementia or Alzheimer's) who have wandered off.

So while I don't do urban searches, some of the same behaviour is exhibited, especially by the evaders. Suspects being chased by police in urban settings would exhibit the same kind of behaviour as prey that didn't want to be found in the bush. They'd probably run as far and as fast as they could and then hide (ideally somewhere familiar to them).

That said, you can improve and test out your tracking skills in urban settings. Anywhere that there is dirt, mud, snow, grass, or puddles you can lay down tracks and practice.

- *Look at your neighbour's lawn and see if the mailperson or newspaper carrier crosses their lawn to get to or from your house. If you see a path in the grass, check to see if the path is silver or dark to figure out if they travel towards or away from your house.*

- *If it snowed, walk down the sidewalk and look at tracks. Based on the step and stride lengths, did the set of tracks you see belong to a walker or jogger?*

If you see a skid mark at the end of a driveway, did someone slip when they were putting the garbage out?

- *What critter left tracks in the dirt and knocked over your garbage? A raccoon? A skunk? A crow?*
- *You can also practice aging tracks in your own yard.*

In "Tracking animals" I'll show you more animal tracks (and I'll tell you what kind of tracks these are on page 195).

Where in the world?

I get asked a lot what are my favourite and least favourite places to track. That's a tough question, and a loaded one. If I say your neck of the woods is my least favourite place to track in, it doesn't mean that it isn't one of my favourite places to visit.

With that out of the way, I'd say that Northern Ontario and Newfoundland are two of my least favourite places to track people. In Newfoundland, there aren't a lot of animals to beat down the bush, so there aren't many game trails. Instead, it's like a maze of garbage scrub to ride through. I keep having to stop and back up on my horse, and find alternate paths to get where I was going. Not only is that no good for the horse, it also slows you down.

In Northern Ontario, it's mainly all-terrain vehicle (**ATV**) and snowmobile trails over rock and swamps, which are hard to track through. There were plenty of spots where the bush was grumpy enough that we couldn't ride our horses through it. Big rocks with overgrown moss also stopped our forward momentum on more than one occasion: those rocks are too slippery for the horses, they can break their legs.

My favourite place to track is probably in ranching country. There are lots of game trails, more dirt, less rocks, and lots of open spaces. In Western provinces, you can ride through the bush because the cows have cut trails: they scratch on the trees, stomp on vegetation, and eat the underbrush. Animals get rid of the garbage brush, so it is easier riding and there is less ground cover for prey to hide in. Cows free-ranging in the bush not only make good trails, but also show you to water, and good crossing spots through creeks. Fields of grass give you a silver ribbon to follow. (Remember, "Hi-ho, Silver! Away!") I probably also prefer tracking in ranch country because I feel at ease there, I have home court advantage, and I have a lot more opportunity for **jump tracking** – which is one of a few different methods of tracking that I'll go over in the next chapter.

Chapter 11:
Methods of tracking

Depending on who or what you're tracking, their physical condition, the weather, and how far behind them you may be, you will probably use a couple of different types of tracking methods. Step-by-step and jump tracking are the most common, and bracketing is a combination of both methods. It's also worth revisiting track traps in this section and what you do when you lose the trail.

Step-by-step tracking

Step-by-step tracking is exactly what the name implies: you find each track before moving on to the next track. In Search and Rescue (SAR), you track step by step, finding each track, to make sure that you don't make mistakes or overlook a sign, as a life might be on the line. Even if you see a path of the same tracks continuing up ahead, you wouldn't jump ahead to them, you'd continue to follow them step by step. Why? You might miss that someone went off the path into the bush down to a stream and left a bloodied bandage. That is important information you would want to relay to the other searchers, that the physical condition of the lost soul has been compromised.

In step-by-step tracking, you have to engage the sign awareness and visual tracking skills discussed earlier. Look up, down, to the side, and ahead. Look high, look low. Use your tracking stick as a guide as to how long the person's step might be and to define the area where the next sign should be and to focus your eyes to the area. Go back and look at "How to look and see: How to find the next sign" on page 20 for a refresher on this.

If you are tracking a wounded animal, you would use the same approach. You want to take care of the animal as soon as possible, one way or another, and don't want to end up following a perfectly healthy animal. You follow every track, step by step, looking for and interpreting sign as you go.

Jump tracking

Jump tracking is what you may have seen me use most often on the television show, but it won't work for beans in thick bush. It's a technique where you want to move quickly on a surface like a road, path or field, to gain ground on the person or animal you're tracking. The name comes from the fact that, even if you saw the track veer off into the bush and come back out to the road, you would jump ahead to the continued trail and not go into the bush to check out what they did in there. Once you find a pattern of tracks down a road that gives you directionality, you make the assumption that the person or animal would continue to travel in that direction. When you find the next track confirming this, you then keep moving in the same direction, looking ahead for more confirming sign, and back-tracking if you jump too far ahead.

On the show, I had the luxury of knowing that my prey had to keep going, and couldn't hide in the bush for a long time like a couple of partridge, so I only used step-by-step tracking if the tracks didn't make sense, or disappeared completely. Especially on my horse, I can gain ground by moving down the road looking for some sign, even if in doing so I miss several tracks. I'm not going to waste time finding every track if I can see where the path is heading. If you can see a path of shine or a path of disturbed leaves (or a combination of both), you can move faster through that section and probably gain some ground. With jump tracking, you also can stay on your horse longer.

Even if your assumption is incorrect and your prey has veered off the path or turned around, you should see that sign cut across your path, especially if you have someone on both sides of the road watching for tracks leaving the road. Then you can alter your tracking direction as needed.

If you're jump tracking and are suddenly faced with a fork in the road, you can use a figure eight pattern to find tracks and determine the direction of travel or to eliminate a path quickly. If I see nothing down one path, I'll try the other one. If the second path shows no tracks, then I have to go back to the last known track and go more slowly, probably using step-by-step tracking.

Jump tracking is often used to track animals. Hunters or photographers don't often care which deer they find, they're simply looking for deer. So even if by moving quickly they don't end up following the exact same animal, they're following a fresh trail, and gaining ground by moving quickly.

Bracketing

Bracketing is again aptly named: it's when you see one track right in front of you and another track up ahead but then need to fill in the gaps between these two brackets and find the other tracks. Where step-by-step tracking would have you keep looking for the next track in a forward motion, in bracketing, if you came across a track up ahead, you could work backwards to find the other tracks. Bracketing is used in SAR, where you're supposed to find every track. Again, the reason behind that is that while veering off the trail, the lost soul may have taken off their bright red jacket (say). With that information, you can inform other searchers that you're no longer on the lookout for someone wearing red. I suppose bracketing is actually the combination of jump tracking and backwards step-by-step tracking, knowing that you jumped ahead and are now going back and filling in the middle, step by step, to learn what's between the brackets.

Track traps

A track trap isn't a method of tracking unless you, as the tracker, have set up the track trap, but this still seems like a good spot to talk about it a bit more. A **track trap** is made at a part of the landscape where, if the prey passed through, they couldn't avoid leaving sign. Track traps are a more proactive tracking method than step-by-step or jump tracking, which are more reactive. Track traps work best if you can estimate the direction and distance of travel, or want to eliminate a possible direction. A tracker can set up a track trap or one can be created by nature.

An example of a track trap set up by nature is a big puddle in the middle of a road, covering most of the road, with a cliff on one side and thick bush on the other (see the photo on page 95 under "Puddles"). Prey won't typically walk straight through a puddle since they don't want to get their feet wet, so you check around the puddle for tracks. As we covered in the section about tracking in different conditions, you can also check the puddle for silt disturbances. If there are no tracks skirting the puddle or going through it, then you have probably eliminated a direction of travel (unless you're ahead of them... which has happened to me before).

A tracker can set up a track trap, too. I remember one time, in the fall, with leaves covering a path, I decided to move the leaves off two patches of the path. I knew that if prey walked on those cleared patches, I'd probably get conclusive sign from their distinctive boot prints. If they didn't walk on the dirt patches, but just walked around them, then I would get corroborating proof that they'd been there from any disturbances in the leaves around the dirt patches. After all, if you weren't the person being tracked, why would you alter your steps around a bare patch of earth unless you were eluding detection? If no sign, conclusive or corroborating, shows up at a track trap, it's time to go back and re-evaluate the direction of travel, because the prey hasn't been through the area (yet). SAR will also use track traps to help narrow the search field.

In this naturally occurring track trap, prey will be forced to the right of the puddle unless they are willing to hop the downed tree on the left. Either way, you know where to find the sign, and it's likely that you'll find it (assuming the prey came this way).

Profiling your prey comes into play in every type of tracking, so I'm not labelling it a type of tracking. Instead, it gets its own full section.

Chapter 12:
The psychology of tracking: profiling

"Curious things, habits. People themselves never knew they had them."

Agatha Christie

I've already said that a student of tracking is a student of human and animal behaviour. You have to know your prey. By understanding more about your prey's usual routines, habits, likes, and dislikes, you'll get a better idea of where to look for them.

Profiling animals

In terms of animals, you need to know the basics, like if an animal is nocturnal or not, whether or not they hibernate, if they are warm- or cold-blooded, what terrain they favour, and, most obviously perhaps, what they eat and where you can find it. Knowing what their predators are and what their typical reactions to those predators are is also good information to build upon.

Are there runs and game trails (paths worn by animals) in the tracking area? Where are the animals' known watering holes? All animals eat, sleep, drink, and excrete, so knowing more about the areas where they do this will help you track them down. Using this type of information, you know that you sure as heck aren't going to look for bats sunning themselves on rocks at high noon, nor are you going to find frogs bedding down on a glacier, or rabbits burying their eggs in the sand (unless they are chocolate and it is Easter?).

You may find moose more often on trails when the black flies have pushed them out of the bush. Near a river where salmon are running, or in a nice blueberry patch are great spots to find bears. Raccoons are more likely to have been the culprits that knocked over your garbage than a mountain cat (and, of course, they leave markedly different tracks that could tell you this).

With basic knowledge of your prey, you can then put yourself in their shoes/hooves/paws/feet and think like you think they would. You combine your knowledge of the species with your knowledge of the area, and with any knowledge you may have about the specific prey that you're tracking. You can begin with what you've read and been told, but then can confirm or disprove certain info in the bush yourself. Seeing is believing.

Humans aren't totally dissimilar to animals you'd track, but there are some big differences:

- *animals can sit still longer than humans*
- *humans leave more ground sign than animals (we have bigger feet and can be lazy and not pick up our feet when we walk). That makes for more damage, disturbance, and transfer*
- *moose will go through a swamp, but humans typically won't.*

Whether we're talking about man or beast, "know your prey" still applies. The more you know about the person or animal you're tracking, the better. With SAR, you get as complete a profile on the lost soul as you can. One of the biggest differences between man and beast is their purpose for being in the woods. Animals are looking for food, water, shelter, mates, etc. Humans could be there to hike, camp, hunt, meditate, or to find mushrooms or fiddleheads.

Profiling humans

We humans are definitely a bit less predictable than our animal buddies, and we can be downright contradictory. Lots of times, we do things that just don't make sense. But, there are enough truisms about people that we can start with to get us moving towards building a psychological profile of our prey even without specific information on them.

Given a choice, we all gravitate to the path of least resistance. It's probably safe to say that it's human nature that we don't want to get too hot, too cold, too wet, too dirty, or too scratched up, and we avoid dark and confined spaces. People prefer to be comfortable and look to avoid undue hardship. After all, when's the last time you saw someone or heard about someone going for a hike in a swamp? We like things easy, so that means:

- *Trails, roads, paths, and railway lines are more appealing to walk down than crossing muskeg or going through a thicket of thorny bushes.*
- *We'll gravitate downhill rather than uphill. However, we might climb to try and get a lay of the land and figure out our direction of travel.*
- *We avoid getting our footwear or feet wet.*
- *We don't like bad smells.*
- *We avoid getting dirty.*
- *Dark places and confined spaces are not our favourites.*

Each of these gives you clues as to where to look for sign just by thinking about how you'd react to certain types of terrain. If I'm crossing a stream, I move from rock to rock. We try to keep our feet dry as long as possible. So, if you're tracking someone across a stream, look on the rocks for dirt or water transfer because the toe of our footwear often dips in the water, and there is sometimes transference of water onto other rocks.

Note: I'm talking in generalities here, but of course there are exceptions. Most kids usually like stomping through puddles. Boys in particular seem to really like the mud and getting dirty. Caves are often more interesting to children because they want to explore these nifty dark places.

A situation can also change your reaction to the terrain. If you're being pursued, you may take more difficult routes or resort to hiding in places you wouldn't usually be caught dead in, just to evade pursuers. In the end, though, any evader starts out being tricky, trying things like going through thick bush and climbing terrain as steep as a cow's face, but eventually, and usually unconsciously, they just default back to the paths of least resistance, and they'll get on a game trail.

- *Of course, it also goes without saying that some people love caves and will spelunk before they hike any day. That's why, in addition to understanding overall human behaviour and the situation that the prey find themselves in, you also want specifics about any human who you're tracking.*
- *In SAR or law enforcement, you look to get as much information as possible about the person you're tracking to further develop the profile. Information about their fitness level, knowledge of the outdoors, profession, medical conditions, habits, height, weight, and shoe size can all come in handy.*
- *Do they have outdoors experience? What gear did/ would they have with them and how long could that sustain them? Are they afraid of the dark or of the water? Are they afraid of heights? All of this info will help you narrow down possible paths of travel or hiding places.*
- *A person's habits can also really help you in tracking. Are they whistlers? Auditory tracking might take over. Are they smokers? Scent tracking might help. One guy I tracked was a big game hunting guide with the habit of snapping branches as he walked through the woods. It's a useful way in guiding to make it easier to find the way out, and it also made it easy for me to follow him. I focused more on top sign than ground sign, because his path of broken twigs was just as conclusive as any tread pattern.*
- *How fit are they? The average person's pace in the bush is one and a half to two miles per hour. If they're cross-country runners, they'll probably cover ground faster than that.*
- *Do they walk with a cane, walking stick, or crutches? Do they have a limp? Knowing this would help a tracker find conclusive sign.*
- *Tracks of a run are different from tracks of a walk, a shuffle, a limp, or even a tired run. You'll know from the tracks if someone is out for a stroll in the woods: their tracks will meander more, and their steps and strides will be shorter because they are travelling slower. Someone out on a mission to get somewhere in a hurry will have straight tracks with longer steps and strides. Someone running away will spend more time turning around – they'll have more erratic tracks, typically off to the side. They might*

run into the bush, walk for 100 paces, come out of the bush, then switch sides of the road to throw off pursuers. Someone out for a Sunday walk wouldn't leave the same kind of tracks, they'd pretty much just stay to the path.

- *If someone is hurt, they will often keep travelling to try and get to medical care faster.*

If you have no other information to go on, just think about what you'd do in the same situation, facing the same terrain, and go where you'd expect to find your own tracks. Try to get into the other person's head...Walk a mile in their shoes.

Once you start finding tracks and/or have sightings of your prey, you flesh out your profile by any past patterns of behaviour of theirs that you've noticed from seeing them or their tracks. Do they have a habit of running along the edges of paths, or hiding in thick bush, or laying down fake tracks? Everything that you see the prey do, or can read in their tracks, tells you a bit about their mindset and their physical condition, including injuries or level of exhaustion. Any of this will help you with profiling and intuiting where they might go or what they might do (or likely won't do) next.

Again, knowing what they like to wear or sounds they make are also good to know. Some people talk to themselves, are whistlers, hummers, gum-smackers, or knuckle-crackers. If you know that, you will listen more actively for it. Same way, like I said before, if you know they tend to certain "loud" fabrics and clothing with Velcro closures, you can listen for the tell-tale sign of the material rubbing or crinkling or Velcro opening.

In the absence of tracks in front of you, the best you can do is look for the obvious place that you would travel. Searchers have also found that:

- *If a lost person can see water through the trees, they will usually go towards it.*
- *If someone is startled and is being chased, they are going to take the easiest path out to get away as quickly as possible. Look for the biggest openings in the woods, and see if there are tracks there. Scan around for large logs and look on both sides of them for tracks from someone jumping over the log or hiding there; see if there is any dirt transfer on top of the log.*

- *People running away from you often want to keep you in sight. Once you go past where they're hiding, they will move, too, so listen and look to the sides as well as in front of you when you're on the chase.*
- *Straight tracks tell you that the person is on a mission and is focused on moving straight ahead. This is one case where jump tracking is useful.*
- *When straight tracks are interrupted by one foot going sideways, or if a footprint every few paces is pointed 45 degrees, the person is watching their **back trail** (the trail behind them – where they just came from) and could be nervous or scared.*
- *If you're following someone's tracks down the road and the tracks show that they keep looking into the bush, then, based on their tracks, they're probably looking for an exit point.*
- *Through the profile, you can also make a few assumptions about the level of tactics you might expect if someone doesn't want to be found. If the person is an outdoorsman and knows about tracking, they'll likely be more of a challenge than the weekend warrior (who may not even think to turn off his or her cell phone).*
- *If someone is a sniper by profession and they decide to hide, they will probably choose a spot where they can get a vantage point on the area.*
- *Some children hide in their closet when they hear their parents fighting. Knowing that about the child would tell you to look for the child in any small cave or culvert, under logs, or any other hiding place.*

All this to say that, you try to think like them and then, on top of that, you layer on any knowledge you have of the person/people you're tracking. I learned a lot about our unconscious behaviours while tracking 118 people on the show. People have very specific habits, different from each other, but you catch on pretty quick if you're paying attention. One girl, every time I saw her, she'd scream, grab her partner and tear off into the bush to the left. She wasn't even aware she had that tendency. I asked her after the show, and she had no clue that she was doing it – not unlike poker players who aren't aware of their tells.

In SAR, building strong profiles on lost souls can make the difference between a Search and Rescue and a recovery mission.

Chapter 13:
Search and Rescue

"The value of a man resides in what he gives."

Albert Einstein

"When people say "it's always the last place you look". Of course it is. Why would you keep looking after you've found it?"

Billy Connolly

"Next to creating life, the finest thing a man can do is to save one."

Abraham Lincoln

Search and Rescue (SAR) aims to saves the lives of adults and/or children who have gone missing (typically outside of urban settings). The missing or the lost are often referred to as the **lost soul**, or **misper** (for missing person). Based on where the search is held, a different team may be called in: ground SAR, mountain SAR, or air and water SAR. Search and Rescue dogs can also be used to aid in a search.

When someone is reported missing, such as a hunter or a mountain biker who didn't return when they were supposed to, or a child who gets lost on a day hike or wanders off from their campsite, law enforcement does all the usual checks first.

They'll talk to the person's family and check local hangouts; they'll find out if the missing person has any friends in the area and talk to them, too. They begin developing a profile of the lost soul as they speak to people who know the person. They'll try to get as recent a place last seen (**PLS**) as possible, so they'll also check surrounding campgrounds, other trailheads, and places of interest. They may also bring in a search dog.

If their checks or the search dog don't locate the lost soul, SAR is usually called. A calling tree is used (the call goes out to one SAR person, who then calls four to five people, who in turn call another four to five people each) to round up 25 to 30 trained searchers. Since SAR personnel are almost exclusively volunteers, the team size and composition on any given search will change based on who is available that day. SAR personnel are from all walks of life, united by the common goal of wanting to find and rescue, as opposed to recover, lost souls.

The search manager sets up a command post at the staging point (close to the place last known or seen), as the SAR volunteers are on their way. Law enforcement officials brief the search manager on the lost soul, giving as many details as possible to help create as rich a profile as possible to help plan the search.

Profile

The search manager is interested in any and all information that might help to find the lost soul(s). The questions break down like you'd expect; who, what, when, where, why, and how. Lost person behaviour also factors into the profile, but we'll get to that in a bit.

Who

Knowing who you're looking for is so much more than knowing their name, age, and physical description. Of course, you also want to know their name, to call out and to write on signs while you're searching for them. Knowing what colour and type of clothing the lost soul was wearing can help searchers find conclusive sign, like discarded or dropped clothing, or fabric snagged on branches. Knowing their shoe size and the type of footwear and tread pattern will help tracks to be identified. Someone's weight will also help in identifying tracks (how deep the imprint), and their height can also help searchers know where to look for top sign.

Knowing the lost soul's level of fitness and experience in the outdoors is important, as are their medical conditions or relevant habits. If searchers know that they are looking for someone unfit, not savvy in the woods, diabetic, allergic to bee stings, or pigeon-toed, with Alzheimer's or a limp, it would modify where to look for lost souls and what type of tracks might be theirs.

If "the missing" is a child, you want to know any particular habits, including what their stress reactions have been in the past (when their parents fight do they have a tendency to hide, run, talk to a doll or stuffed animal?). Are they whistlers or hummers? Do they shuffle their feet, or tend to kick rocks down a path? Are they slowpokes? You want to know anything and everything that will help you find them faster.

What and why

Finding out what they were doing in the woods (also answers why they were there) is also helpful. If it is known that they went hunting for moose, there are areas they are more likely to be in. Same thing with someone picking berries. Knowing if they were equipped to spend the night and what gear they had can also help identify a campsite, dropped items, or places they may have stopped.

When, where and how

Once you have a good idea of *who* is missing, the search manager can layer on the information they have about *when* and *where* the lost soul was last seen, and *how* they were travelling (on foot, bicycle, ATV), to help map out the areas where lost souls are most likely to be found.

Planning the search

Once law enforcement calls in SAR, briefs them on the situation, and provides the profile information that they've collected, the SAR search manager (search coordinator or search master), working out of their own command centre or search base (usually a motorhome), then takes over the search. SAR basically runs the search for and with law enforcement, and together the search managers may change the strategy or search area along the way as new info comes in.

Based on what has been ascertained in profiling the lost soul, you can imagine it would completely change the search area. The radius of the search area for a small child would be smaller than the search area for a mountain biker, or a hunter on an ATV. Fitness level would determine how far someone may have travelled, but also how much rough bush they could handle before they resorted to the path of least resistance due to exhaustion. That said, just because someone is a marathon runner, don't automatically assume that they will have travelled farther than a hunter. Marathon runners are not used to lifting their feet over logs, roots, and rocks, but seasoned hunters are.

The search manager begins by determining the theoretical search area. They make some mathematical predictions on where the lost soul might be based on where they went missing, when they went missing, and how quickly they might have travelled. Statistics from similar incidents are also factored in.

The search manager starts by putting a dot on a topo map at the PLS or the **LKP** (last known position or **PLK**: place last known) depending on the scenario. For example the PLS might be a bank machine video, and the LKP or PLK might be where his pickup truck was found (assuming he drove it there). The place last known is used usually for air searches, like the coordinates that were called in with a mayday before a crash.

Going out from the PLS, the search manager determines the radius of the search area based on average speed of travel. On foot, the general rule for adults travelling through the bush is 1.5- two miles per hour. This area is referred to as the **search area** or **area of detection** (AOD). Ideally, they'd want to set up a perimeter along the edge of the AOD based on the PLS, and any part outside that area is referred to as the **rest of world** (ROW).

Then the topo map is studied for natural barriers that would narrow down the search area or AOD to an **area of search** (AOS). Natural barriers can also change the type of search (cliffs might require rope rescuers, lakes might require water rescuers). The map is then divided into search areas of higher and lower areas of probability of where the lost soul may be.

The search manager makes calculations as to the:

- **probability of area** *(POA), which is the likelihood that what they're searching for will be in that area*
- **probability of detection** *(POD) or the likelihood that they'll find the search object, if it is in the search area, and the*

- **probability of success** *(POS) or the likelihood of finding what they're searching for, given the POA and POD (POA x POD).*

Formulae exist for all of these, but this is just an intro to SAR in a tracking book as opposed to being a SAR training book, so we'll keep it simple and not get into the math of this.

Search teams aren't just sent to the areas with the highest POA; they're also sent out to eliminate lower probability areas. A lake may be covering part of the search area, so the shore of the lake has to be checked for tracks going along or into the water. As a SAR team member, your purpose is to help find the person or narrow down the field of search.

Searchers also need to know what the weather was doing in the area when (and since) the person went missing in order to be able to age tracks better. Search managers will consult weather stations; they'll ask locals and ranchers what the weather was around the time the lost soul disappeared; and they'll consult park rangers, who often chart the weather in their parks.

While all this profiling and planning is going on, the SAR volunteers are arriving at the staging area (not the PLS). The teams assemble at a staging area so that tracks from the PLS won't be obliterated; also the PLS or PLK may not be vehicle accessible. There can easily be 50 vehicles at the staging area, including the SAR command post vehicle, law enforcement vehicles, and even an ambulance on standby.

As a volunteer, you're expected to show up ready with your duffle bags of search gear so that you're prepared for the unexpected. I often had rubber boots, hiking boots, hip waders, a helmet or hard hat, rope gear, life jacket, layers of clothing, gloves, sunglasses, safety glasses, a first aid bag, tracking-specific gear, and, of course, the SAR 24-hour pack mentioned under "Preparedness."

Next, the search teams are put together based on the searchers available and the jobs that they're best suited for. Team leaders or search captains are designated for the various search areas as well. If you're trained as a spotter, you may be sent up in an airplane or helicopter. You might get sent out on a **quad** to sweep trails at a higher speed. People with rope skills are typically kept at base camp so that, if another team finds the lost soul stuck on the side of a cliff or injured from a fall over a cliff, the rope rescue folks can be dispatched quickly.

The search manager then decides the order of the searches and how they'll be done. Some will be asked to follow a trail reactively; others will proactively try to get ahead of a trail. For example, a number of tracking teams will go out with people trained to track and navigate. Some teams will do trail sweeps, but others will go in vehicles to other trail heads to get in front of where lost souls might be, to ask anyone they come across if they have seen the missing person out there.

Regardless of what team you're on, you log in when you arrive and you log out when you leave the search base. Once assigned to a team, you stay with your team. Leaving a team can make it ineffective, as everyone on a team has a role. You can put the search in jeopardy by not following simple communication protocols.

Sometimes you never make it out on the search because the person has been located. One time, I was one and a half hours into a briefing at the staging area, when one team member arrived late (she couldn't get off work earlier). Once she heard the description of the person and his clothing, she realized that she had seen someone like him hitchhiking on the road on her way in. The RCMP went out, and confirmed that it was him. Turned out, he was lost, ended up on a road and decided to hitch home instead of trying to make his way back to his car at the trailhead. He had no idea a search was being formed to find him.

It can be a couple of hours (or more) before the search manager has the search area or AOD determined, the search planned, and the teams organized, briefed, and ready to go. Of course this can be frustrating as a volunteer, because you just want to get out there and find the person as soon as possible. You know that not all searches and rescues are successful, and many turn into body recoveries. Time is always of the essence, but every minute of planning can save the search teams hours in the field.

Before you go out and start searching, you need to be aware of (and honest about) your own limitations. You have to be prepared to be out there all day, so if you have a sore ankle, maybe that day you shouldn't be part of a hasty team, but instead you should take on another duty at the search base, so that you don't hamper search efforts by needing a rescue yourself.

The other thing you should do before setting out is to notch a mark on the bottom of your boots or take out a lug, so that it is easier for trackers to eliminate your tracks if they come across them. This is especially important if you're part of a Hasty Team.

Hasty Team

In SAR, the tracking team is called a **Hasty Team**. It is a three-person team including a tracker, a navigator, and a person in charge of communications and first aid. There can be several Hasty Teams working at the same time in different areas.

The tracker has to focus on just that: tracking. The tracker is at the front of the triangle formation for the team. The tracker can't be worried about navigation, so the navigator is there to focus on where the team is and where they have travelled. Similar to that, you don't want your tracker distracted by communications coming in from the command centre, so you have a communications person. Teams also have to check in once an hour and give their position so that the base/search manager can track their position. That way, if a team goes out of radio contact, they have an LKP and time for them, and can start a search for the searchers, if need be. Since tracking is exhausting, every person on a Hasty Team is trained in all three roles. After two to three hours of tracking, or any time you start to get eye strain, it's time to switch roles. When your eyes are tired, you will find it more difficult to focus, and you can get frustrated. By rotating jobs, the tracker is always fresh. (On the television show, I had to stay focused on the tracks ten plus hours a day, which is hard to do.)

As the tracker (or any Hasty Team member), you're looking for human sign. As mentioned in "Methods of tracking," you're also trying to find every track, using step-by-step tracking and sometimes bracketing. You sometimes get a tread/sole pattern of the lost soul to follow; otherwise, once you have a conclusive track, you can also take a photo of it on a digital camera to refer back to during the rest of the search.

There was a whole section before on interpreting sign, and that doesn't change for SAR. When someone's tired or carrying a heavy load, you'll see deeper tracks and more drag in the tracks. As well, they'll be more likely stick to the path of least resistance. If they're tired, you'll see more stumbling and more negative impressions from stubbing rocks. If you see two left foot imprints in a row, someone might have stubbed a toe and is now hopping on one foot, but you need near perfect conditions to find that stuff.

You're concerned with finding sign that gives you important indicators of physical condition, like blood or bloody bandages. Similarly, if the stride is long (they are running), and that is a sign that their hips, knees, and feet are working fine. If they knelt down to get a drink, their back and knees are ok. If they climbed a cliff, their arms and balance are ok.

You may want to go back and review the section "How to find the next sign" on page 20 for what was said about tracking sticks. In summary, a tracking stick can help you find the next sign, by using the lost soul's past step length (as marked on your tracking stick with an elastic) to gauge where the next sign might be. The measurements for track length and width also marked on the tracking stick help to conclusively identify tracks. A tracking stick can also be used to focus your eyes down to the area immediately around the point of the stick, making it easier for you to find the next track or sign.

A tracking stick also helps you mark tracks. When you find a conclusive track in SAR, the tracker marks it by circling it in the dirt with their tracking stick and then flagging it as a left or right foot. If it is a right foot, you put at least a two inch-long line off the right side of the circle at the bottom of the track. A half-moon below the track is used to mark a partial print, and again you use a line to mark which foot the partial track is from.

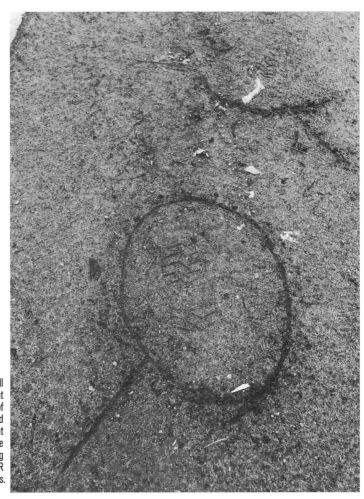

A conclusive full left track is at the bottom of the photo and a partial right track is above it, according to these SAR markings.

It's more often that you are marking partial tracks than full tracks.

There is another less-known use of a tracking stick, and that's to whack in the shins any navigator or comms person who starts to move up beside you or, heaven forbid, in front of you, as they may step on tracks and destroy them. Actually, I'm sort of kidding about the whacking, but there is some truth to it. The tracker has to be out front for obvious reasons. It should really go without saying, but while you're tracking, never destroy the tracks you're tracking. That's where the marking of the tracks helps in SAR: you don't ever touch a track with a circle or partial circle around it.

While the tracker is the point man, narrowly focused on the immediate foreground, the navigator and communications person are flankers, behind the tracker a bit, looking at everything except the tracks. They scan ahead and to the sides for a backpack or other discarded or dropped items and obvious top sign. They are also responsible for looking up. If you were tracking alone, you'd have to go slower, and remember to look up at the different levels for top sign and even higher up in case someone has climbed up somewhere or thrown something up into a tree.

If a backpack or a piece of clothing that matches the description you've been given is found, the comms person calls in the position and a description of what was found. The search manager will confer with law enforcement. Depending on the time of day, the weather, and the importance of the piece of evidence found, they'll ask the team to rope off the area until they get there or they might just have the team "bag it and tag it" and take it with them. Either way, SAR team members do not manhandle evidence without being directed to do so because they don't want to disturb any possible fingerprint evidence.

Teams asked to mark off the area would do just that, and would then wait for forensics to take over the scene. The team would stay and assist the officer(s) with anything that they needed. Depending on what was found, the search manager may shift more trackers to that position, having the current team continue on the trail, or have another team be called in and briefed to they take over the trail.

If asked to bag and tag an item, the Hasty Team will often first take a digital picture of the item's location, then they will use gloves to place items in Ziploc bags, marked with permanent ink pens. A quick written statement of what was seen and done would be recorded.

If inclement weather is on its way, teams may be asked to protect sign they've found. In the 24-hour backpack, you carry an 8'x10' tarp; with that and a couple of sticks, you can protect evidence from the elements quite well.

As much as I've talked about tracking, on SAR missions, you often don't have tracks to follow: you just have the PLS and/ or the PLK and maybe a direction of travel. It could be that weather has erased the tracks, or that all of the usable tracks have been stomped on if SAR wasn't called in until the third day or so of a search. In those cases, you aren't tracking as much as searching. You use the profile of the person, along with your knowledge of the terrain, as well as lost person behaviour to narrow your search. If SAR is lucky enough to have an actual boot print belonging to the lost soul, they draw it up with measurements and that goes out to all of the search teams.

Typically, you search from noon until dusk, go home to sleep, and come back again in the morning to search again the whole next day. Sometimes you stay overnight on certain trails of the lost soul's potential path, but since SAR is all volunteer-based, many people can't stay the night. The length of the search on any given day also depends on the terrain and weather. In the winter, you only have light from around 8:30am to 4:30pm, and weather is a concern for the lost and the searchers. That said, depending on the search manager and the situation, you might track 24 hours a day, straight through the night, especially if you're hot on a trail since people tend not to move at night, it's quieter, and with the right lighting following the tracks can be relatively easy.

When your search manager calls off the search for the day, or another team is coming in to replace you because the day is getting long, or the weather is getting grouchy, there are a couple things to do before leaving. If you were on a trail of tracks, you'd mark it with ribbon so that you still have a direction of travel and have a place to start tracking from the next day. You'd also set up string lines at trails with big yellow tape (like crime scene tape) with signs on them that say, "If you are John Smith, we are out looking for you and will be back here at 8pm." If you go back there at 8pm and the missing person is not there, you change the time on the sign and continue your search. One string line can save putting a searcher on that path, freeing them up to search elsewhere – you just hope that the person you're searching for can read your message.

Even if the weather is getting bad, in SAR they say: "There's no bad weather; only bad clothing" and they encourage preparedness for all searchers.

Tracking and search methods

Under types of tracking methods, we've already been over step-by-step tracking, jump tracking, and bracketing. You don't use jump tracking in SAR: you use step-by-step, and sometimes bracketing, but either way you're looking for every track, whether you find them in order or in reverse. These methods are slow, but you can't afford to rush and miss important information about the prey's condition or location along the way.

In addition to tracking methods, there are several search patterns to consider. There are so many different patterns (fan searching, expanding spirals, box searches, and circular patterns) that it would be a really long chapter if we included them all. We'll stick to line searches and critical spacing. By the way, the reason that these are search patterns and not tracking methods is because they make for a lot of feet wrecking any possible tracks.

A line search is a police tactic used as a last sweep of an area, when they aren't worried about tracks. You've probably seen a line search executed on television, where a bunch of locals help to sweep a field, all walking in a row, looking at the ground in front of them. It is a technique to find anything and everything; any kind of evidence, and sometimes bodies. It could be that they're trying to locate a murder weapon thrown into the area when they have already apprehended the criminal, so his tracks are irrelevant. Or it could be that the lost soul is known to be dead, so it is a body recovery mission, where speed is not as urgent.

The problem with line searches, other than the difficulty in getting that much manpower, is that searchers rely on their peripheral vision to see things to the sides of them. That makes the **critical spacing** (CS) (spacing between searchers to maximize the efficiency and effectiveness of searches) very important, otherwise small items can still be missed. A military line solves that problem by having two lines, one in front of the other, where the searchers are offset.

With any pattern, the spacing of the search members is important, and has to be adapted to what you're searching for, while factoring the terrain. One technique is called the **Northumberland rain dance**. In this method, you set down an object similar in size and shape to what you are searching for and determine the maximum distance searchers can be apart to still be able to detect such an object. If you are looking for a lost child, you would set a backpack down, to simulate a child in the fetal position. Two people stand on opposite sides of the pack and walk away from the pack until each can just barely see the pack. Now both people continue walking around the pack a half circle (both moving clockwise or counter clockwise), always keeping the pack in view, moving closer to or further away from the pack based on lighting and terrain and vegetation. Then the minimum and maximum distances between the searchers and the pack are averaged, to determine the critical spacing for the search in that terrain. For example, if searchers have a maximum distance of ten yards, and a minimum distance of six yards, their average is eight yards, and the critical spacing will then be 16 yards between the searchers (such that there is only a maximum of eight yards between the object and a searcher).

If you're looking for a knife, you would use the same process, but replace the pack with a knife or similar size object. Because the method changes with terrain, vegetation, and lighting, every team has to do the Northumberland rain dance in their own search area to come up with their own CS, and if any of the factors listed above changes significantly in the search area, the CS has to be recalculated. If there are culverts, coulees, or snowed-in areas, you'd have to investigate them closer up because lost souls could have gone in for shelter, or to hide, or may have fallen asleep, or worse. You'd check the base of pine trees covered in snow (as there's a sheltered spot by the trunk), and you'd check every lump in the snow larger than a human.

I don't think I was ever told why it was called the Northumberland rain dance, so I asked Guy Kerr, a friend I met through SAR. Guy and I met at a SAR fundamentals skills basic tracking course many years ago. He's a 25 year veteran of the Calgary Police, a SAR instructor, a search manager, and a contributing author of the Emergency Response Institute's (ERI) SAR Skills book, the Initial Attack Search Management book, and the ERI Team Leader Manual. Not only did Guy proofread this chapter to make sure the content was current, but he also had the answer I was looking for about the Northumberland rain dance. He told me that when the Lockerbie plane crash happened in the U.K. a method was needed to do effective and efficient searching without having searchers lined up an arm's length. Arm's length apart spacing meant that many searchers were required to cover the area, so it took too long and was a waste of resources. By going to critical separation, searchers are used more wisely. The method was developed by two mathematicians, Dave Perkins and Pete Roberts, who were SAR folks from the Northumberland area, and they were coordinating the search for body parts as a result of the crash. Since it rains so much in their area, and they were often circling an object in the rain, it got to be known as the Northumberland Rain Dance. While the distance is not exact, the concept allows for mathematically calculable 50% POD (probability of detection), but is in most cases more than 50%. Guy has run scenarios where the object used was a pack and the clues in the field were considerably smaller (like a one-dollar coin) and their team still had a 100% POD.

Here's Guy in his SAR jacket, keeping his tracking skills sharp at a recent practice search.

Purposeful wandering is a slightly more random pattern of three to four people in a line narrowing and widening out their critical separation as the terrain and vegetation dictates. You keep track of the person on your right (the person on the far right is following an assigned compass bearing), and only go as far away from them or near to them as needed, in order to be able to see the object you are searching for. Again, this is a search method not a tracking method. You would move in as a team and out as a team to make sure you can see all of the land in between you and the next person and not miss something because you're too spread out, or waste search time because you're too close together.

Under "Tracking in different conditions" we covered "Urban tracking," or should I again say urban searching. Urban searching is very specialized, used following natural disasters to find people and bodies, or to find a missing person, typically the very young and very old. The good thing with urban rescue, especially following a natural disaster, is that people usually want to be found, which isn't always the case when you look at lost person behaviour.

Lost person behaviour

Lost person behaviour is an offshoot to the psychology of tracking. It's a combination of understanding the person's profile, the terrain and weather they're facing, and their preparedness for both. It's based on statistics of past incidents as well. For the most part, you ask yourself, "If I were the person who made this track in front of me, where would I go next?" Then you check the obvious places you might go for sign. So you have to get into people's heads.

Things get a little more complicated when you're tracking someone different than yourself. Tracking a child is different than tracking adults; women tend to do things differently than men; medical conditions can throw a whole new wrench into your profiling as well.

Men often have a sense of pride or a macho thing going on. They're thinking: "I'm big strong and tough and I'll bull over things." So they jump over logs until they cramp up. Women aren't trying to prove anything to the logs or rugged terrain. Also, while guys think more on the run, women stop and think things through and strategize more (and are more likely to hide).

All people, especially when they are tired, will tend to choose the path of least resistance. They prefer trails to thick bush, downhill to uphill; and they are attracted to water, as it looks like an opening in the bush. Hikers and children are more likely than others to travel uphill, whereas hunters and the elderly notoriously will travel downhill. People will climb a hill to try and get a perspective on where they are.

Also, none of us walk straight lines in the bush; we all tend to curve one way or the other. Is it because one leg is longer than the other, or we step around obstacles in the same direction every time? No one really knows, but if you know in which direction you curve, you can correct it.

The majority of people will get on trails to try and be found, and will stop travelling after 24 hours; about a third may even travel at night their first nights. A large majority of adults will be found within five miles, and children within two miles, of the PLS or PLK.

Let's look at a few more differences between types of lost souls.

Children

When looking at the terrain, remember that children will opt for routes that adults wouldn't choose. You have to view the terrain from their perspective. They'll fit easily in and through places an adult wouldn't even consider attempting. Children also fall asleep in the strangest places, so you can't assume they won't be somewhere: you have to check everywhere.

Children, especially ages one to three, may not even know they're lost; they're investigating. They have open, innocent thoughts: everything is fun and new and interesting. They'll wander and continue to wander aimlessly. They have little to no sense of direction, and are often more concerned about finding a place to nap. In a meadow, they'll go pick flowers, find a little hill in a sunny patch, and take a nap. Once they realize that they're lost or they start to get scared, they are likely to start to cry and fall asleep, probably huddled under a tree, not thinking that they will be nearly impossible to find that way.

Slightly older children, say ages three to six, are still very interested in exploring the world around them, and can be easily distracted by something they see and lose all concept of where they are/were and where they were going. They may also be interested in a nice place to nap. However, many of them have been warned not to talk to strangers, so if they are being searched for and hear people yelling their name but they don't know the person calling them, they may hide from them.

Even older kids (ages six to twelve) may not only avoid searchers because of stranger danger, but they might also be afraid that they're going to be punished by their parents because they got lost or ran away. Especially on day two or three of a search, kids are scared that they're going to meet with mom and dad's worst punishment when they're found. That makes them evaders, with hiding being their top evasion technique. They may only accept help if they get cold or hungry, or if it gets dark. Let's face it, it would be scary having a bunch of adults yelling out your name while they search for you. Yelling, even by the best-intentioned person, just doesn't sound nice.

Youth aged 13 to 15 will usually respond to searchers' calls.

Overall, when searching for a child, you have to check every hiding place and consider paths an adult wouldn't. You're also trying to find children faster, before any harm comes to them.

With an adult you aren't as worried, figuring they can take care of themselves; but kids are so innocent, they wouldn't see the danger coming.

Most children are found within two miles of where they were last seen, and maybe because it is easier, about two-thirds of lost kids will travel downhill when given the chance.

Elderly, mentally challenged, and the despondent

With the elderly and mentally challenged, you can also be dealing with the same type of reactions as with children, except with the elderly you'll also have to deal with the fact that they could be hard of hearing and/or forgetful. Also, the mentally challenged will be more likely to hide or stay in the same place and do little to help themselves.

People with Alzheimer's will not cry out for help, nor will they reply to searchers (only in 1% of cases will they call out or reply). They are wandering looking for home or for their place of work, even if their home or the workplace that they're looking for is from 20 years ago and is 300 miles away. In urban settings, they might take a bus and get off five miles away from their stop, thinking that they're home. They're probably going to go to their last known address, or where one of their kids live. They also never forget their life's work, so if they were in construction, check out nearby construction sites and hardware stores. Back to the bush, people with Alzheimer's just keep going until they get stuck; the only thing that helps searchers is that those lost souls tend to walk in circles. Also, according to a number of studies, people with dementia are more apt to be found if searchers follow the initial direction of travel. They are usually found within one mile.

The despondent person is not lost. They are looking to be alone to contemplate suicide and will not respond to searchers. They are typically found close to civilization, at scenic spots or in an open area surrounded by trees. They do not travel far.

Bikers, hikers, hunters, and climbers

Mountain bikers, from my experience, are predictable in that they refuse to turn around. They assume the trail will eventually lead somewhere. One guy I searched for got lost after he missed a turn in the trail and just kept going, even when he knew it wasn't the path he thought it was. When we found him, he had half a bottle of water and was wearing spandex shorts and shirt. He'd gotten a flat, didn't have a spare and had to spend the night. He was pretty uncomfortable when we found him; there is only so much you can do to keep yourself warm when you haven't packed layers and you've got no fire starter.

Hikers will start out on a loop trail, but when they get tired, they decide to cut straight across the loop as a short cut back towards the trailhead. Once they get in the bush (usually without a compass), they get turned around, and take any likely-looking trail. They think they're on their way home, but more often they've actually turned the wrong way. Soon, darkness hits, and they're three miles away from anything they recognize.

They typically get found within five miles of the PLS or LKP. One difference with hikers is that they tend to be more willing to travel uphill when lost than hunters, for example, who will almost always travel downhill. Hikers also tend to stay to trails and will travel further than others.

Climbers and hunters are usually better equipped, and have maps and a knowledge of the area, but an injury or sudden weather can get them in trouble. Hunters are often prepared to spend the night with the gear they have on their backs and in their packs. Hunters may not be lost at all, but if they know they won't be able to get their kill out of the bush before dark, they'll tend to make a shelter when it starts to get late, and they'll walk out at dawn. Most hunters are found within five miles of the PLS or LKP.

After day one, evaders, and hypothermia

No matter who you're tracking, almost anyone can get to the point where they think the searchers that are there to help them are actually somehow out to get them, so they become evaders. Your profile of them should help you to know what level of evasion tactics they might use. Military personnel are trained to evade and hide their tracks; hunters are more bush aware, know how to camouflage themselves, and know where to travel and hide to make it hardest for you to follow or find them.

When people get cold, in extreme cases, they can get hypothermia; the elderly are more susceptible to this. As hypothermia progresses, a small number of people start taking off clothing because they start to feel warm. If it is winter and you're doing a search and you start to find layers of clothing, unfortunately, you're probably too late to help the lost person.

After more than one day of someone being lost, if they didn't have a lot of gear or supplies with them, you also want to look for signs of foraging for food and water, and making shelter. On day one and day two, you're looking for an upright human walking about, trying to find their way out or trying to find food. You may find a shelter on the second day. By the third day of any search, you know time is limited and you're searching even more aggressively. Most children and adults by now will be feeling pretty low (emotionally, as well as physically low on energy) and will probably be huddled under a tree. Too much after that and, unfortunately, you're thinking more about body recovery.

My SAR experience

When I took my initial SAR training in the Turner Valley area with Foothills SAR, there was an initial introduction to tracking and SAR that covered preparedness, survival, navigation/ orienteering, tracking, lost person behaviour, tracking sticks, marking tracks, search patterns, and radio communications. After that I took the two-day course called the Fundamentals of Mantracking: The Step-By-Step Method, developed by Ab Taylor and Donald Cooper. As SAR we're also expected to have our first-aid certifications up to date.

For the SAR missions that I was on, I wasn't there as a tracker most times, but I was part of a Hasty Team. I've been in about 30 Search and Rescue missions with the Foothills SAR, with varying results. Some were easier searches than others, and some lost souls even walked out of the bush just when we showed up to search. Because it's a volunteer job, I missed a lot of searches because I was working those days. We had a pretty good record of finding lost hikers, bikers, hunters, and children; but some we didn't find in time, and some we never found. There was one time we were on a search for a hunter and we never found him, but we found his car at a trailhead. Hopefully, he's sipping margaritas on a beach in Mexico.

Another time, we found a ten-year-old Scout who was happily having a little adventure on his own. He'd gotten separated from his pack and got to a creek, but didn't want to get his feet wet, so he went up about a mile, and found a place to cross. He was unaware that the creek was curved, so when he thought he was on the right trail, he ended up on a trail straight east. He didn't much care though. As a Scout, he was prepared to stay the night: he had a small tent, food, and water, and we found him the next day.

On the one and only urban search I was ever called in on, a kid went missing in the town of Okotoks in Alberta. We were asked to do the search, but as searchers, we do not enter houses, garages or sheds for safety reasons. We asked the homeowners to search their houses and outdoor structures thoroughly. They came up empty-handed. Turns out the kid had gone to a neighbour's house, where he used to talk to the neighbour while he fixed up his car, and the kid had fallen asleep on the back seat of the guy's car. The whole town was out looking for him, along with SAR, but we were all down by the river.

We learned from that one that even though everyone wants to get out of their house and join the search, you have to get them to seriously check all of the bases on their own property very thoroughly first. This means looking in obvious spots and comfy places in the house – kids can curl up and fall asleep in a closet, or under a bed, playing with stuffed animals.

Speaking of curling up, a friend of mine's Auntie was around two years old when she got separated from her sister on their way to their Grandma's in the Ladder Lake area of Big River, Saskatchewan. As Jeanette tells the story, her Auntie had taken a wrong turn and was lost: she was wearing a silk dress and no shoes. Once her family realized that she was missing, a search team was called, and the mill was shut down so that the workers could help look for her. They had tracking dogs coming from Regina, but before they arrived her Auntie was found in Brownfield meadows. When she was found she said, "The big black puppy helped me." She said she'd curled up and slept with it overnight. It was no puppy; it was most certain that it was a bear. She was one lucky girl!

On a less happy note, I was asked to help out on a search for a young boy in the Greater Toronto Area. He had run away because his parents had taken away his Xbox. I got there on day three of the search and was asked to help coordinate the volunteers. Three to five hundred volunteers were showing up daily, but lucky for me, the people who did the volunteer coordination before I got there did an awesome job, so our job was easy. A former prey of mine from the television show, a police officer named Dave, was on the case, too. The search involving SAR was eventually called off, as volunteers had searched their AOS. In the search area, there was an area controlled by the police that the volunteers were not to search. The boy was found in that area, by hunters; it looked as though he had walked off a trail, crawled up a tree, and sadly had fallen out.

Police rightly think about a lost soul differently than SAR does. The police can't limit themselves to thinking that a child (or adult) just wandered off and got lost in the woods. They also have to follow other leads, speculating a possible abduction, like in the case above, that the boy had been lured away by another Xbox player. The police can't narrowly focus just on the woods for their search; they have to do all of the urban search and follow up on tips about vans in the area and such.

I still get contacted to help in searches now and again, but I haven't been with SAR for a while; the show kept me too busy. I'm still honouring the protocol that I only go to track if I've been called out by the RCMP.

In addition to the SAR work I've done, there are also the 118 people I tracked on the show. Maybe because there aren't that many (if any) SAR people who have tracked that many people, I'm now considered a bit of an expert. But this isn't about boasting, I'm just happy to have been able to track across so much unfamiliar terrain (SAR work is usually just in your own "backyard"), and I'm pleased with my "capture" rate, given that the prey I chased didn't want to be found.

There is no ego (or at least, there shouldn't be) in SAR. It's not glamorous, there's a lot of waiting, and not only might you not find the lost soul, you might never see hide, nor hair, nor track of them. That doesn't make your role any less important, as your team may have eliminated part of the search area that allowed others to be redeployed to find the lost soul in another area. Also, you may never get to use the majority of skills you're trained to use, and trust you me, you've taken a lot of training and want to put it to good use. It can also be a thankless job, with little to no recognition and not enough funding for search efforts.

You're there to work as a team, as part of the SAR team helping law enforcement. It shouldn't matter if you helped find the person or if you helped eliminate an area of search. Who finds the person is not important. I guess I'm not painting all that pretty a picture, and maybe I'm doing my best to not make it sound all that exciting, because we want SAR members who aren't glory hounds, we want people dedicated to helping other human beings, who are satisfied with having a part (even a small part) in getting people home safe to their families. For me, working with SAR as a volunteer was an amazing experience for the training, for the wonderful people I met, and for the knowledge that while others were sitting on their couches hearing about missing people, I was out there trying to do something about it — no matter what the outcome. Life wasn't just happening through the television screen for me.

If you're interested in SAR, either in doing the actual searches or teaching the education programmes to kids that help to make SAR searches unnecessary, I encourage you to contact one of the national, state, or provincial SAR organizations. I've listed the national ones in the reference section. You can tell them that I sent you.

Ideally, instead of helping SAR members get better at tracking (as they are already quite good), we hope that this book might help with the prevention of SAR calls by educating you (and having you educate others) on how to not get lost and how to help SAR teams find you if you do get lost.

Chapter 14:
Don't get lost! Are you lost?

"I've never been lost, but I was mighty turned around for three days once."

Daniel Boone

"It's a lot easier to be lost than found."

Sarah Dessen

"No matter how far you've gone down the wrong trail, turn back."

Turkish proverb

We all get lost at some point in our lives, but some of us, like Daniel Boone, just don't want to admit it. The sooner we accept the possibility that it could happen to us, the sooner we can start making the appropriate plans in case it does happen.

What you can do before you leave home

To avoid getting lost, or to increase your chances of being found, reread "Skills of a tracker" especially "Preparedness" and "Paying attention." Pack your pack accordingly and try to expect the unexpected. At a bare minimum, make sure you have a good map and a compass and that you know how to use them.

Check the weather before you set out. If some rough stuff is headed your way, stay home (or at least be prepared with more gear in your pack).

Also, anytime you're going into the woods, tell someone where you're going, and/or leave a note, and/or leave your route highlighted on a map. Frequent outdoorsmen will even laminate a map of their favourite areas and use an erasable whiteboard marker to mark their planned route and their expected return time.

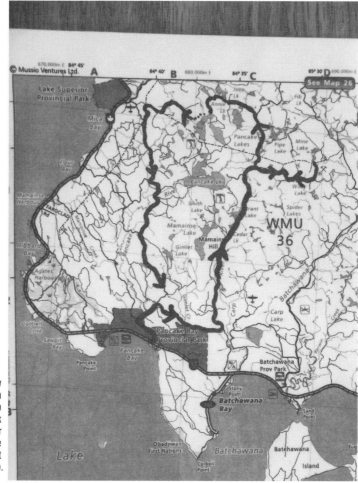

A dirt biker drew his route on a laminated map with a black dry-erase marker (just in case rescuers might need to find him).

It's also not a bad idea to put a pair of your underwear or a sock (that you wore all day) into a Ziploc bag tightly sealed in the freezer. Scent-tracking dogs can use this to help find you. Tell your family members to hand the bag, sealed, to searchers, and not open the bag otherwise they can contaminate your scent. If you have kids, ChildFind Canada recommends that you do this even if your children don't go in the woods – it's a quick ounce of prevention!

What you can do out on the trail

The most obvious piece of advice is to go to areas you know, and/or to stay on well-marked trails. You shouldn't change your mind and decide to explore a new side trail if you didn't mark that as a possibility on your map back at home.

Keep looking back at the path behind you, to know how to get out later. Notice major landmarks like a big composite rock, a large log, a small creek, a muddy section, etc. You can even use a digital camera to take photos of your back trail if you're worried you might not remember which path to take out.

When you're going off trail, snap small pieces off of the ends of branches or even bring flagging tape with you to tie a small piece onto a tree every little while (but if you do, make sure to take it down when you leave).

If you think you're getting turned around, stop, look around, and start tracking yourself backwards.

If you need help

If you're officially lost or hurt and need help, don't panic or feel bad. It happens to the best of us.

You can try the advice of an unknown author: "If you're lost in the woods, play Solitaire with a pack of cards. Someone is sure to show up and tell you to play the red jack on the black queen."

Stay put

Jokes aside, the next most important thing to do is to stay put. Stay on a trail if you're on one. If you're close to a trail and can make it there, go to it. Other than that, staying put is better than wandering around, and it will increase your chances of being found. There is an educational program called "Hug-a-tree and Survive" that we used to teach in schools a lot more when we had more funding, with just that message: if you're lost, grab a tree on the trail and hug it or stay beside it: don't wander.

Contact someone

If you can, contact someone. Try your cell phone and try calling out for help, or blowing three consecutive blasts on a whistle. If you reach someone, try your best to describe where you are and your physical condition and tell them to contact the police. If no one answers, or you're out of range, and you don't have the luxury of a sat-phone, this is where I think new technology really can help out.

There's a cool gadget called the "SPOT Satellite GPS Messenger" that can help you get out of a tight one. You preset the people who it will contact via email or SMS if you press the HELP button, and it gives them your GPS coordinates (within 20 ft). There is an SOS button that will alert an international emergency response center to have local emergency crews dispatched to your location.

It's only a couple hundred bucks, which is nothing if you consider what a safe return home (for you or your loved ones) is worth to you. It might be good for tracking your teens in urban areas as well (only they have to press the button to let you know where they are).

Aside from the HELP and SOS buttons, there's an OK button that is pre-programmed to say whatever you decide to use as a check-in message, like: "I'm ok, just letting you know where

I am." If you have the SPOT Connect you can send whatever message you like by pairing it with your Smartphone. Either way, the people that get your message will be able to link to a website to see where you are on a map plotted by the GPS coordinates when you sent the message. If they hit the I'm OK button a few times along the way, contacts could see the trail of GPS points.

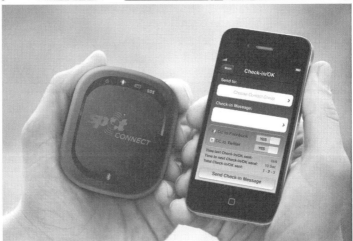

The only catch with the SPOT is that you have to remember to bring it and fresh batteries with you on your outings.

Get seen

While you're waiting for someone to come and find you, you'll want to make yourself as visible as possible, from the ground and from the air. You can use a mirror as a signalling device: move it back and forth in front of you, across the horizon, because air searchers might see that flash of reflected light, even when they can't see you. Hang out bright pieces of clothing, unless you need them to stay warm, so that searchers can easily spot them. If you can't make it to a trail, try to throw stuff onto the trail to make it easier for people to find your general location. They'll stop to pick it up, radio it in, or talk about it, and you can use your whistle to signal you're there if your voice is hoarse. If night is approaching, try to start and maintain a signal fire. Once your fire is strong, you can add some moss or leaves to create a lot of smoke.

Find shelter

Depending on your situation, you'll need to start thinking about finding or building shelter (while remaining visible), staying dry and warm, and finding food and water. Maybe I should reverse those last two, because you can't last much more than three days without water, but you can survive weeks without food. Speaking of food, don't eat anything in the bush unless you're 100% sure that it is edible.

Stay positive and safe

To keep animals away and to comfort yourself, you can whistle, sing a tune, or talk to yourself. Remind yourself that everything is going to be fine and that you will be found soon: stay positive! If you hear a noise in the woods, make a noise, so that searchers can find you more easily, or to scare away animals.

Kids!

Everything in this chapter applies to you too (except lighting a signal fire), including telling someone where you're going, staying on the trails, and, if you become lost, staying put, being visible, and staying warm and dry. If you want to learn more or make sure that your friends learn the skills to not get lost, or to get found easier, you can ask that your school or community group (like Scouts/Girl Guides) gets an instructor in to teach the Hug-a-tree and Survive program, or ask your parents to buy the book *Lost in the Woods: Child Survival for Parents and Teachers*, by Colleen Politano.

More than anything, though, if you ever do get lost, you need to know that no matter how grumpy you've seen your parents in the past, you will NOT be in trouble if you're missing, not even if you ran away on purpose. You will NOT be punished. NEVER hide from Search and Rescue teams, even if they sound a bit scary calling out your name.

Chapter 15:
How not to be found: Evasion

"What are you doing?" Sarah Connor says, as Reese turns on loud machines around them in an industrial setting and starts moving. "Cover, so he can't track us." Reese replies.

Terminator (1984 Sci-fi movie)

If prey is using **evasive** or **anti-tracking techniques** to not be seen or found, the tracker has to take a special view of the tracking situation. Evasion is used when the goal is to slow down the tracker or completely bamboozle them, so that the prey have time to get away.

Most evaders think they're smarter than those they're trying to evade, but lucky for us, they rarely are.

On the television show, obviously, people don't want to be found: they want to reach the end point before the time limit or before I catch them. That's a luxury I have that most trackers don't. Hiding is one of the best evasion manoeuvres, but on the show, because they and I know that there is an end point and a time limit, my prey have to keep moving or they will run out of time. That allowed me to jump track more and step-by-step track less.

I loved when people got creative in their anti-tracking techniques, it was pretty fun. It showed me that they were thinking. It kept me alert, more aware. It also made me know that they were worried, but more importantly, I knew that I was gaining ground on them, because these techniques take so long. With some techniques, I just wonder, "What were they thinking?!" Like when they spend a lot of time making false trails where I'm not likely to even see those trails, or when they "erase" tracks, making it that much more obvious that someone passed through the area. I can almost see their little mental hamster wheels a-spinning: "Why don't we use reverse psychology...wait he'll be expecting that...let's use reverse, reverse psychology." By the time they figured out what they were going to do, I was busting out of the bush towards them.

Sure, every kind of evasive tactic can work to some degree, but some are better than others. Once you've seen backwards walking once, it takes an experienced tracker only a few tracks to notice what's happening. Travelling through unexpected terrain like the thickest, meanest parts of the bush, will not only leave a lot of sign for the tracker, but it will be tough going, and again waste the prey's time. It typically slows down the prey more than the tracker.

You have to think of the opportunity cost of any evasive manoeuvre. Are you confident that it will pay off by slowing down your pursuer by more time than it took you to create it? Sure, any time you get me off my horse, you've slowed me down, but it won't be for long, and I'll just be more determined to catch you, especially if you tried to mess with my horse.

Regardless, I have seen all kinds of evasive techniques. To tip the scales even further in trackers' favour, let's look at some techniques that can be used against us:

- *Camouflage or concealment*
- *Avoid leaving sign or hiding sign*
- *Change the sign they made (false directionality in tracks, or making you think that the tracks you see aren't theirs).*
- *Make false sign (false paths/false directionality in trails)*
- *Hamper the tracker's movements.*

Camouflage and concealment

Blending into your surroundings is a great evasive technique. If they can't see you (or hear you, or smell you), they can't find you. Camouflaging face, skin, and clothing really helps you blend in. A white flash of a hand in the bush is like the flip of a whitetail deer's tail. Camo gloves are good to avoid that. After changing your colour, you can also change your shape to blend in better. The goal is to break up the outline that your pursuers are looking for, and it hides your movement better, too. Whether you stick some branches on your hat or go for the full ghillie suit that the military wear on stealth missions, it will change your form and make you harder to spot.

Staying out of sight by your speed of movement and position relative to the skyline is also important. Slow, quiet movement is the most difficult to detect, and typically leaves the least sign. If you think you might have been spotted, either flatten yourself on the ground or tuck yourself quickly behind a tree and stay frozen there for a while. Stay low enough to not skyline yourself on a ridge; stick to the tree-line to blend in with the vertical trees.

Prey that stay hidden for long periods of time will frustrate any tracker and can cause the tracker to give up, thinking that they might be on the wrong trail. I've tracked a lot of ladies who were pretty darn good at hiding like a pair of partridge in the bushes.

The last way to stay hidden is to travel where you aren't expected to. No one expects people to choose to travel through a swamp, and no one wants to track you through one. Same goes for thorny thickets or nasty bush.

Avoiding leaving sign

There is almost no way to not leave sign, unless you've got a fancy jet pack or wings. That said, there are places to travel that are harder to find sign, and other places where sign will be erased by others or the elements.

- *Staying on trails or roads allows your tracks to blend in with others, and people will step on yours as well. I find it tough to track on well travelled paths because there are a ton of tracks, which can make it a real guessing game. The downside is that being on trails makes you more visible. Similarly, crossing*

*through a field where cows are being wrangled will
ensure that any tracks you've made are obliterated
by the cattle.*

- *Walking in rushing water (creeks, rivers) won't leave
  trails, but you have to be mighty slick to not leave
  transfer when you exit the water.*
- *Where there are waves hitting the shore (sea, lake,
  river), if you walk at the water's edge, the waves will
  erase your tracks. But make sure the wind is blowing
  in the right direction and that the tracks are being
  erased. Again, the downside is that you're highly
  visible if you're walking along a beach or the edge of
  a river.*
- *Treading lightly through vegetation (or anywhere) will
  also minimize sign but not eliminate it.*
- *Running through leaves beside a road or trail is more
  visible than tracks on the road or trail.*
- *Travelling on rock and hard ground leaves the least
  sign.*

Hiding your own tracks

It is near impossible to hide your own sign by anything you
do. Any brushed-out track is conclusive sign. Sweeping away
tracks easily covers the tracks, but it's hard to cover the signs
of covering the tracks. In order to properly cover up five feet
of tracks, you'd have to sprinkle leaves and dirt in a natural
fashion – but you'll leave ten tracks in your effort to cover up
five. Dragging a tree or branch behind you can cause more
disturbance than your walking would have, including wherever
you chopped down the tree. One couple who I tracked
dragged a small tree across the sand, which had the effect of
highlighting a passage in a book that you don't want people to
read. You may as well point an arrow, strike up the marching
band, and say, "Here I am." It's time-consuming, never really
pays off, and it helps me conclusively determine that I'm on
the right trail. I start paying more attention when things are off.
And the absence of tracks tells me heaps.

Changing your sign

Through chasing 118 people, I've seen a bunch of ways
that people try to change their sign to throw me off their trail,
including:

- *Changing footwear (so I saw two new tread patterns)*
- *Duct-taping reverse soles to boots or making backwards shoes to make it look like they're walking in the other direction*
- *Putting carpet on the bottom of their feet, twined on*
- *Taping t-shirts to shoes to disguise tracks*
- *Bagging feet for a while*
- *Wearing neoprene socks with no tread – they make for nearly no tracks on hard ground*
- *Crawling down a beach instead of walking (but they left knee and hand prints)*

The problem with a lot of these "tricks" is that the additions that they put on their shoes either didn't stay on very long, or slowed down their travel. Or instead of walking down a road in them so that I might be fooled, they stepped off the road and went up a hill or walked in the bush where it was obvious that the sign I was seeing was human, even though the treads were different. If you want to try and trick me, you have to show me the tracks!

One cool attempt was putting horseshoes on their feet – but the only thing is that they didn't travel the way a horse would, so I caught on pretty quick. I gave them an 'A' for effort, though.

Another decent idea was putting tennis balls on the end of walking sticks. This is great for gravel, to hide that they were using walking sticks, otherwise, every second step, I'd have seen a hole in the ground. But in snow, it simply left a bigger print than just the walking stick would have. I'd also recommend that, if you're thinking of using this technique, a colour more subtle than brand new, bright yellowy-green tennis balls might be a better choice.

Making false tracks

If you're following someone who doesn't want to be found and the tracks are too good to be true, or the sign is really evident (like someone really churning up the leaves or pine needles in an area, or leaving bits of thread on branches), as a tracker an alarm bell should be going off in your head.

While it's possible that the prey got careless or tired, or that you startled them and they took off in a hurry not worrying about the tracks they left, it's more likely that you're being played the fool. Of course, there is also the chance that your prey started second-guessing their second-guessing and reverse psychology-ing their psychology and decided to leave good tracks hoping that you'll think they are false tracks. Problem with that logic is that I'd usually follow the false tracks until they loop back or I could see them loop back: if they were real tracks, they wouldn't have slowed me down at all.

Alternatively, if the false tracks are down one part of a fork in the road, you can move to the other path to look for conclusive sign, having eliminated that first path. Evasive manoeuvring early in the tracking, like right off at the start or at the first fork in the road, is probably one of the best times to do it, because the direction of travel hasn't been well established yet. I'd lose a lot more time following false trails looping on and off paths at that stage of the game, because I'd need to be pretty certain of a direction of travel before leaving.

If a tracker is looking for two people (or more), i.e., at least two sets of tracks, a technique like **bombshelling** isn't a bad plan. That's where you split up and travel apart for a while and then regroup. It backfires badly, though, when you don't preset the rally point, or you lose each other. A variation of this is when prey choose to split up and talk by walkie-talkies as they pursue separate paths. The problem with this variation is that the walkie-talkies can beep or make other noises that might alert the tracker to the prey's position because they stand out in the bush.

I've said it already, but walking backwards is not very deceptive to a skilled tracker. It's quite obvious to even a relatively new tracker. Aside from the shorter, less straight steps and strides, the toe kicks and heel marks are different. It's also much slower, so it's ineffective, because your tracker can gain ground on you.

The best technique is to set false tracks on obvious trails, especially going around corners, and then go off-road at a different angle. Unexpected direction changes make trackers slow down and pay attention. It will buy you some time, because the tracker won't be able to see your trail loop back, and they may jump track assuming your original direction of travel. Soon enough though, when they lose your trail, they'll go back to the last known position and go about things more carefully. You'll be sitting pretty if weather has come in since and cleared the signs of your actual travel.

Hampering the tracker

If you are tracking someone who really doesn't want to be found, they may be looking to hurt you to slow you down – but that's only in extreme cases where criminals are involved or in military applications. In this section, we'll cover more recreational methods of hampering a tracker, like ones I saw on the television show.

Everyone knew that I track on a horse, so a lot of the ways prey tried to stall me involved messing with my horse. The strange thing is, though, I wondered if they'd ever seen a horse or knew anything about a horse, because it beat me why anyone would think that dragging a log across the path would do anything except hurt their lower back. I either had the horse step over the log or take an extra second to go around it. I knew that I was gaining ground, because I knew it took them more than a couple of seconds to move the log.

On the show, one of the better roadblocks was one by the team that put up old telegraph wire. Not sure if they wanted to take my head off or knock my hat off. I stopped to take down the wire. Even though it slowed me down, the team told me later that it took them 25 minutes to put up the wire: it delayed me by only ten minutes.

Using the terrain against me and my horse was also a common technique, but if it slowed us down, it slowed them down, too. Also, lots of prey found out only too quickly that horses could handle some pretty hairy terrain. That said, horses aren't fans of:

- *loose, rocky, steep hillsides*
- *large smooth rocks, which are too slippery for horses; they can easily break a leg on them unless they've got corked shoes on*
- *fences – they may as well be walls to horses; that's where prey can gain a lot of time on us.*

Trying to scare or irritate my horse was another common tactic. Prey bought a deer whistle to mess with the horse. Others purchased wolf urine in the Yukon, hoping to make my horse skittish. Others tried cougar piss. They spent time pouring it about, but the horses didn't even notice. One person purposefully stepped in bear crap, thinking horses wouldn't follow her. She was wrong. It's hard to throw a horse off its game unless the real predator is there. Even then, I've passed close by grizzly bears, and all the horses did was snort, they didn't even slow down.

The closest anyone came to bugging the horses was the team that strung up a **bearbanger** booby trap with fishing line and a flare (a bearbanger explodes to make a really loud noise to scare off wildlife). I saw that "cobweb" from far away and I remember my sidekick in that episode, Phil Lemieux, even saying, "That's an awfully straight spider." Maybe if we'd been off in La La Land they might have gotten us, but we're pretty keyed in when we're tracking.

Auditory techniques

Concealment means blending in not only in appearance but also in terms of the noise you're making. If you can use other noise to cover the sounds of you moving, like running when an airplane flies overhead, you will probably remain concealed.

False sign can also be auditory. One expensive counter-tracking technique used against me was leaving a pre-recorded voice recorder playing in an area opposite to where they were headed. I could hear voices coming from two directions. I followed the nearest sound, which ended up being the tape recording, but was back on the real auditory trail pretty fast.

Not so evasive techniques

Sometimes by accident, the prey dropped things like lighters or binoculars, and especially when there isn't a lot of sign around, I'm happy to see those things, because they are conclusive sign. What boggles the mind is when prey leave panties, a feather boa, or cards. It's all conclusive sign, and it's like they're baiting me to find them faster! Like my friend Joni (from the Yukon), the only female guide I had on the show, said to me: "They're pretty dumb to leave their panties out like that, as any man would be sure to track and find them!"

Tips for evasion

I don't really want to help anyone be more evasive, but overall, it's a question of being invisible by blending in...in appearance and being silent. So pick clothes that are quiet (not nylon) and camouflage yourself with items that match the season (all camouflage clothing is not created equal; colours range from sand-colour to dark green, and there is even a greyscale urban camo). Move quickly to try and get as much territory between you and your tracker(s) without leaving any more sign than you have to. Pick carefully the areas you walk on (unless you're on solid granite rock, you're going to leave some kind of sign, even one bruised piece of grass). You also have to decide if you'll sacrifice moving slow and leaving no tracks, for moving fast and leaving a full trail. Change your direction in a place the tracker will see it, but wait until you've gotten around a bend or corner to change directions. At every Y, put down fake tracks (but don't take too long doing it). Split up and regroup to throw off the tracker, but make sure you have a preset rendezvous point. Stay away from roads and settlements, they make for easy tracking. You can use the road as a guideline. If you know the road is going in the direction that you need to travel and you can stay in line with it from the cover of the bush, you can save yourself some time by not having to take compass bearings.

Some additional random tips for you: keep a steady pace. Don't exhaust yourself too soon – slow and steady wins the race. Don't wear cotton: you sweat, your clothes get and stay wet, and then you get cold. And don't drink the water (drink only what you brought with you unless you packed water purification tablets). It's hard to be evasive when you're freezing cold and your teeth are chattering or you've got the scoots.

Now that we've given up some tips to prevent being tracked, here is the opposite: things that can help with tracking.

Chapter 16:
Tracking aids

"There are no shortcuts to any place worth going."

Beverly Sills

Especially after discussing ways prey can try to evade you a lot of people wonder: "Can anything make tracking easier?" I'll just say: to each his/her own. Tracking in groups, using technology, and/or tracking with animals (horses, dogs) all have their advantages and disadvantages.

Tracking in groups

Some people think that tracking in groups makes tracking easier. Thing is, you're poor company when you're tracking. You can't carry on much of a conversation or be a tour guide. Similarly, you can take a course with a group of people and learn the basics in a couple of weeks, but then you have to do it yourself to get good at it. It's not really a team sport. Hasty Teams in SAR are the exception.

On the television show, the occasional guide would come along who had a solid knowledge of the area. Those guides helped me to eliminate routes of travel and sped up the tracking. Having an extra set of well-trained eyes that can search one side of the road and doesn't expect me to entertain them is a real help.

That said, you could probably tell from the show that the local guides they gave me as sidekicks really varied in quality. Some were chosen because they knew the area, some seemed to be chosen because they could ride a horse. Others must've trumped themselves up pretty good on both accounts, but when push came to shove (or chase), they weren't much help with figuring out possible directions of travel, they couldn't track for beans, and it was clear pretty quick that they hadn't ridden in decades.

Tracking with someone who can ride, knows the area well, can help eliminate paths of travel, and can figure out directionality is pretty cool. They just can't be a prickly pear or a yappy lap dog who grates on your last nerve. Tracking with someone with a good sense of humour really helps, too.

Bottom line, it can be really helpful tracking with skilled people: then I don't have to worry about missing something in the area they're searching. Otherwise, I'd rather just do it myself.

Tracking technology

People ask me a lot if there have been any "advances" in tracking technology. While there are things out there that can help in searching or help in very specialized circumstances, overall tracking is just a skill you gain with practice. If you really want to be good, you have to work at it: there is no "app" to shortcut the learning.

Infrared devices

Helicopters equipped with FLIR (forward-looking infrared) can pick up body heat. During the day, FLIR is less useful because everything is emitting heat, even the trees. At night, heat emitted by deer and elk will also be picked up when you are looking for a lost soul. Clearly I'm no expert, and I don't own infrared cameras or glasses, but there is an application here for Search and Rescue teams, if they received more funding, to give them access to this technology.

Night vision lenses

"Why don't you catch the prey at night while they're sleeping?" is one common question I get about the television show. There's a couple reasons for this. Like I said before, it's more difficult to track at night and it's much slower. Unless you can see your prey's campfire smoke and can track that, night tracking just wouldn't be a lot of fun. You can cover so much more ground after day-break. The other main reason is that it is exhausting to track (and to evade), so everyone deserved a break at night. In particular, you have to remember that my horses have to stop for eight hours a day. They need that time to eat and rest. Anyhow, I know that I'm more used to a night's sleep on the ground than the prey are, so I'll have an advantage on them in the morning.

Since I wouldn't track at night, I wouldn't need night vision goggles. Also, if you've ever worn them, you know that your depth perception is totally off and you have no peripheral vision. Tracks would be distorted and the prey could be walking almost beside you and you could miss them. They're for searching, not tracking.

Sound enhancement technology

Under "Sensory tracking: Hearing", I mentioned that I don't think that sound-enhancing technologies would work so well in the woods. While the thought is good, the woods are not quiet places, and I really don't know if a sound magnifier could enhance noises selectively. If a mouse is 20 feet away, you don't want it to sound like a small train coming at you. Also, if the prey aren't talking and instead are using sign language, military hand signals, etc., then good luck enhancing only the noise of the prey snapping branches and not that of the moose stepping on twigs.

Global Positioning System (GPS)

As I said under "Preparedness", I still prefer a topographical map and a compass to a GPS, but that could be because I don't have a real fancy GPS. It's great if your GPS combines your topographic map and compass in one, I suppose, but I never had to worry about my compass or map needing new batteries and stopping working. I also find the GPS screen pretty small, and it's hard to get a good idea of the overall lay of the land. Look at how many people have driven off the road and into the bush following GPS directions. I don't want to be spending so much time looking at a GPS screen that I don't notice I'm about to ride off a cliff. At the very least with a GPS, you could record a good spot to bed down for the next time you're out that way camping. It's a marvelous tool, as long as you recognize its limitations.

Digital camera

I think a digital camera is a great thing to bring along tracking if the display screen is big enough. You can take photos of your map in case you lose it, the tread pattern of the footwear you're following, of evidence or tracks as you find them in SAR, your back trail to find your way back, and you can take photos of wildlife too.

Plaster casting

If you're collecting evidence or proof (usually a law enforcement task), you might want to take casts of tracks you see. If you're finding all kinds of bear tracks and wolf tracks, it might be pretty cool to cast those tracks: you could end up with a really neat collection. But you don't cast tracks when you're on the move tracking someone. With digital cameras that can record the tread pattern you're looking for, I can't think of why you'd cast a track unless it was for evidence or a new hobby.

Tracking with animals

For the most part, tracking with an animal is a big help. The ultimate helper in finding lost souls or prey is a dog that can scent track. In most situations, the prey wouldn't have a chance, and we'd find lost souls a lot faster (assuming we could get the dogs on their trail soon enough and the weather was cooperating). My horse is probably the other best helper I could ask for; horses see and hear so much more than us. I think looking for people with a trained hawk would be awesome, but I'm not sure that's ever been done. Watching other animals can also help you in your tracking efforts, too, and I'll add some more to what I already said under "Interpreting sign: by category: Disturbances."

Wildlife behaviour

Watching for animal movement can help you track people or other animals.

I've watched deer before to figure out the prey's movement. If you see deer run into a field and then stop and look back, they give you an idea of where the perceived threat is. I've seen a deer lift up its head from grazing, jog 25 yards, eat a bit more, and then look backwards. This kept up for a while. Turns out there was a grizzly bear in the woods, and the deer was keeping the same distance between it and the predator, and keeping track of the bear as it went. Now had it been a cougar or pack of wolves, the deer would have probably kept running. Deer and elk will treat a human like they do a bear – they will keep a certain distance from you and keep an eye on you, but won't keep running.

Ground birds like grouse and partridge will fly up if scared or agitated. It's a clear indicator that something is moving through their area. In the HBO mini-series Generation Kill, there is a great conversation about how the birds help them to identify where the enemy is not hiding. The journalist in Iraq with US troops says: "I was thinking, those trees, over there behind us, maybe the guys who fired at us were in them." One soldier replies: "As much as I appreciate Rolling Stone's tactical input I'm confident in the birds." The journalist, sounding rather stunned says: "Birds?" The other soldier explains: "Anything moves in those trees and the birds don't sing."

Grouse (left);
Blue Jay (right)

One of my guides, Curtis, once told me that scavengers often follow people. So when a raven flew overhead one time when we were working together, we used it as corroborating sign that we were going in the right direction. If I was tracking near water and gulls were around, I'd watch them for the same reason. They wait for humans to drop food or garbage, and often hang around until that happens.

Birds, chipmunks, and squirrels also call to signal threats. Thing is, they make all kinds of noises and I am not trained enough in bird- or squirrel-speak to know how to interpret it. You can usually tell the sound of an irate bird or squirrel, though, and it could be that someone is too close to their nest for comfort, so that can help give up intruders too.

Tracking with horses

Only a damn fool ignores his horse. Horses offer so many advantages while you're tracking. Granted, there are some disadvantages with them, too, but let's start with why I like tracking with a horse.

Advantages to tracking with a horse

- *Horses are a great mode of transportation.*
- *Being at a height off the ground helps you to see a lot of tracks and sign, like disturbances, from farther away. You also get better visibility to see into the brush. You can often see 50 yards ahead as opposed to ten if you were on foot. It's easier to look farther to the sides for entry and exit points along a road, and to see over tall grass for disturbances where someone has jumped in.*
- *They can help you track longer distances without fatiguing yourself: they do the walking and they carry the packs for you.*
- *It's a lot faster (and I hate walking).*
- *Because you can track faster, you can take more liberties with checking a few trails – lope down each trail 100 yards, and check for tracks. You're losing only 30 seconds or less instead of three minutes or more.*
- *Once you find a conclusive trail, you can go faster on a horse to follow the trail than on foot. A slow lope will have you gaining ground on your prey.*
- *I don't have to pay attention to my feet and where they're landing – I can focus on the tracks. The horse takes care of where you're going. If you were on foot, you might walk yourself right into a tree because you were so focused on the ground, but a horse won't get in a wreck like that. When you're following a trail of shine, you need to keep your eyes on it or you can lose it. Being on horseback, you don't have to look away. If you were jogging to catch up on your prey while following shine, you wouldn't be able to keep the same focus because you'd be worried about your footing, and how tired you were getting.*

- *Horses are great on rolling hills and big hills. They're also really good in three feet of undergrowth that is a tangly mess for humans. They can walk through two and a half feet of water no problem; that much water would push a human downstream. On a horse, you don't even get your boots wet through most water. Horses can swim too (but you would get your boots wet then). Horses can also get through up to one and a half feet of snow, or six to eight inches of mud pretty easy. Humans' boots are just made to gather mud, so I prefer to keep mine out of it.*
- *People underestimate where horses can go. That gives me an advantage. Horses can go up a surprisingly steep hill, but the rider has to grab some mane between their ears and hope the horse's head doesn't hit them in the face as they climb.*
- *Horses help you run down prey, quick. Also, being chased by a guy on a horse is more intimidating than being chased by a guy on foot.*
- *Horses can also get you away from danger in a hurry in case you surprise a bear, cougar, or wolf. Any prey in the rut or in rut (mating season when animals get frisky and aggressive) is unpredictable, so being on a horse is a good way to stay safe. Horses really can save your hide. Nine times out of ten, a bear won't bother something as big as a horse; and if it is the tenth time, a horse can outrun a bear – a human can't. If a bear does catch up to you or surprise you, a horse kick will do some damage to the bear; a human kick will lose you your boot, you'll probably just pull back a stump. The best a dog could do is slow down a bear, or distract it so that you can get away: a bear might back off if it got sick of a dog's barking.*
- *As mentioned in "How it all started", watching a horse's head and ears can help you figure out where prey or predators may be lurking. They're an extra set of eyes and ears and usually see and hear things before us. Their senses are just more in tune. If a horse keeps looking back down the trail, the prey is probably there. If one ear keeps pointing up to a bluff, that's probably where the prey is hiding. One time on the show, our prey was twenty feet from us, one horse flicked one ear back, and the other looked behind him. A couple of minutes later, both horses*

looked in the same direction again; we didn't see a thing. The prey told us later that they had run across the trail and jumped into the bush. We should've heeded the horses. That said, I've ridden horses within twenty feet of a grizzly that the horse never saw. Horses can miss stuff too, especially if the wind is not in their favour.

- *You really can learn all kinds of info from horses' cues. Even more specifically, when they turn their head, they've seen movement; both ears also go straight up, like a pointer dog's ears. They turn their ears towards the direction of a noise. A snort usually means a wild animal that they don't like and that they can smell but can't see, like a bear, is nearby. A snort combined with them moving is telling you that it's a wild animal or something that they can't categorize: whatever it is, they have decided that it is a bit too close to them, so they have to move. They'll just turn and look at elk or deer – they won't snort. Young horses that shake their head, drop it, and back up a bit are telling you that something is going on and that it may be time for you to get off or hold on tight: they're confused and close to that fight-or-flight response. When the ears go straight back, it means they're pissed off and could be getting ready to buck, so you might want to take a deep seat.*
- *Some horses can see really well at night, but others are night blind. You only know by trial and error. When riding after dark, I've had a horse stop dead and I couldn't tell why, so I got down to look and, sure as heck, there was a gate there. You really don't know if a horse is night blind until you ride a trail and they bonk right into a tree (then of course it's a disadvantage of tracking with a horse).*
- *Horses have different likes and dislikes, and if you spend enough time with one horse, you begin to learn those likes and dislikes and can use them to help you. I'd know if my mare had sensed a bee's nest, and I could tell from her cues if it was a woman or man up ahead on the trail (even if I hadn't seen them yet). She was raised by a woman, and acted different around them than she did around men. My old mare also hated moose. If she sensed a moose, she'd start looking for a way out...and if she decided it was time to leave, I'd better be hanging on!*

Notice the horse's ears – straight up like a pointer. If the horse's ears are turned left, I learned to look left.

- *My old mare could scent-track cows. She'd find the scent and follow it. She'd sniff trails at a fork in the road, find the right scent, and we'd be back on their trail. She was a smart horse, and she knew what we were out looking for. Her name was Blue Amy, but I called her Horse. She was a grulla (a Spanish word pronounced gruya), the colour of a mouse, and had a black line down her back with zebra stripes on her legs. I had her for 19 years. She'd come on a whistle, would stand there all day if you dropped the reins, and would listen to commands. I could ride her all day and never have a bridle on her head. She was a good rope horse, too. She was a great horse all around.*

- *If I had the same horse every time I tracked people, I bet the horse would learn to scent track, too. I wish I had had the same horse on every show, but hey, it was more of a challenge for me to get used to a new horse in every location.*

Blue Amy (aka Horse)

Animals leave less vegetation disturbance, but they aren't concerned about not making tracks.

Disadvantages of tracking with a horse

As I said in the previous section, some horses are night blind, and finding that out when you're trying to get someplace at night is a real disadvantage, and there are a few more I can think of as well.

- *Horses can spook, some easier than others, and how they get spooked can be random. Bearbangers would spook most horses, but you don't know what they'll be frightened of. Like I mentioned with Horse, my old mare would take off in the bush with you holding on for dear life because she didn't like moose. That's a real disadvantage if you're tracking in moose country.*
- *You have to concern yourself with the horse's fatigue, even if you feel fine and aren't out of breath.*
- *An endurance runner can outrun a horse if they're really in shape and don't have to stop for water (if they're wearing a CamelBak pack for water). Horses have to stop for eight hours a day. They need that time to eat and rest, and you have to water them once or twice a day. They can easily walk or trot most of the day, but as soon as they start running, they tire quickly.*
- *Each horse is different; some are more used to loping, and lope a couple of miles a day. Cattle horses and ranch horses work cows almost daily, so throw them into a lope and they can go a long ways. Dude horses or outfitters' horses never run: they're trained to walk because of the safety aspect of having novice riders and kids on them. So, like a box of chocolates, you never know what you're going to get when you get handed a horse to ride. They all get a bit clumsy and miss steps, too, when they get tired and that can make for an unexpectedly bumpy ride.*
- *There are also terrains that horses just can't handle, even if you keep reminding them to pick up their darned feet. One horse I had, Corky, didn't want to get his feet wet. I've also had to slow down and do a lot of detouring to keep a horse safe after it got stuck in the mud of a creek bank. Fences are like brick walls for horses. Dense brush, really steep inclines or large smooth rocks are all terrains where humans have the advantage. You never know how deep*

muskeg is and you could get into quite a jackpot with crap like that, so you have to get off and lead horses. Similar to that, most horses don't do swamp worth a darn.

- *Horses can snort and whinny at the wrong moments and potentially tip off the prey that you're about to ambush them. One reason for that is that horses get herd-bound and like having their buddy. Without them, they get nervous; they're not used to being alone. It's like two girls in high school who do everything together. After they walk to school together in the morning and they split to different*

homerooms, they have to start texting each other as soon as they're apart. This happened to me in the Big Muddy (in the Saskatchewan Badlands). As soon as the horses were apart, they'd whinny. This was both an advantage and a disadvantage. The advantage was that you could split the horses apart on purpose so that the whinny of one would send the prey running right towards the other.

- *Horses can hurt themselves or lose a shoe, and that will slow down your tracking. One of our horses crossed a snowmobile bridge, slipped a leg between two slats, and lost a shoe.*
- *If you're not an experienced rider, walking hurts your behind a lot less than riding.*

The advantages of tracking on a horse far outweigh the disadvantages – in my mind, anyway. Granted, anything that can help you with tracking has its limitations. Even if you were tracking on a quad, it would have its drawbacks. Horses are great, but they don't always react the way you want them to. Dogs seem a little more consistent, and their sniffers are second to none.

Tracking with dogs

One good dog is worth three good horses. As a cowboy, I always had a dog with me. He was company, and I'm not sure why, but I'd talk to him more than to my horse. I'd tell him to get the cows moving and I'd even use dogs to gather the horses.

Dogs love you unconditionally. They'd throw down their lives to try and protect you from a bear. I've even let my two border collies, Buddy and Jessie, turn my living room into a rumpus room littered with chew toys and bones – they're family.

Dogs aren't only man's best friend, but without hesitation, they're the best trackers out there. If we'd had a trained dog tracking with us on the television show, it would've almost been cheating: the prey really wouldn't have had a chance.

Since I'm no search dog expert, I consulted my friend Constable Roger Bellerose of the Edmonton Police Service Canine Unit for this chapter. His dog Indy, a German shepherd, is a general service dog trained in tracking, building and compound searches, protection and apprehension work, article searches, and more. Indy is also trained in drug sniffs for a variety of narcotics.

Thousands of police dogs, like Indy, working across the continent, have been trained to detect different substances like narcotics and explosives, and also to track people. There are also cadaver dogs and water dogs, trained to detect dead bodies. The water dog is even more specially trained to smell bodies in or close to the water. If it was a SAR scenario, a dog trained in dry land and surface tracking would be called out first. If they followed a scent trail to the edge of a cliff, with water below, SAR might then send a water dog out in a boat.

Outside policing, dogs have even been trained to smell mold or termites inside house walls, and even more amazingly, to detect breast and lung cancer by smelling people's breath.

Dogs' brains have a much larger portion devoted to smell than humans, and they have more scent receptors. Humans have five million scent receptors and dogs have over one hundred million. So a dog's sense of smell is significantly better than a human's. (It makes me wonder, though, if they have such great sniffers, why do they insist on sticking their noses so close to another dog's butt when they meet?)

Certain breeds with longer noses have more scent receptors and are better known for scent tracking. For example, dachshunds have around 125 million scent receptors and bloodhounds have 230 million. The noses of bloodhounds, beagles, and German shepherds top the good sniffer list, which explains why we've never seen a poodle or a wiener dog sniffing luggage at the airport.

In police work, bigger breeds are preferred for apprehension and protection work. In Canada, you see a lot of German shepherds and Belgian Malinois on K-9 units because of their size and 'cause they're also well-suited to the weather.

Also, male dogs are "better" at scent detecting, though the reason why is not known.

Dogs can be used to apprehend a criminal who has fled the scene of a crime, or to help find a lost child in Search and Rescue. Dogs use scent tracking if law enforcement has a piece of recently worn clothing (like following the scent off of a worn sock) of the prey or lost soul, whereas air tracking is used when they're looking for a human, but don't have a scent article.

If you can get a dog in the area last seen and help it get on the scent trail within hours, it's great, because that scent only lasts so long. The dog handlers are trained to move in a zigzag pattern with the dogs, to help them find the air scent. It's called "winding" a guy. Once they've got something, the zigzag pattern narrows until the dog can follow the scent on the ground right to the person. That's because dogs also track people through ground disturbance, in addition to odours deposited on things they've touched, and/or the wind or airborne scent from an individual.

We lose 50 million skin cells a second, and it is our dead skin cells, or "rafts", that get released into the environment that make up our individual scent. Even if the smell of your feet is really different from the smell of your armpits, it's the same to dogs. When dogs track people, the "track picture" that they follow is a combination of the individual odour of the prey, scent from their clothing and footwear, and earth or ground scent from the crushing and bruising of the ground and vegetation.

Dogs can usually perceive scent for up to 14 hours, but odours do evaporate. Affecting a dog's ability to track scent is anything that dries it out (wind or warm temperatures), scatters it (wind), dilutes it, or washes it away (rain). The sun's ultra-violet rays also speed up how quickly individual scent disappears.

Terrain affects scent too: trees, shrubs, and dips in terrain hold scent better. Frost and snow also can preserve or not hold scent: frozen grass that is walked across leaves little scent. A scent trail could even be frozen in the fall but then be detected again during the thaw in spring.

Chemicals or other strong scents can also temporarily deaden a dog's sense of smell, but once he is taken to a clean environment, he can recover in less than a minute.

The best conditions, then, for dogs to scent-track are when: the weather is mild and there is little to no wind; the ground is warmer than the air (like at night); the ground is moist; there are a lot of trees and bushes around (in the bush); there are no other strong odours present; and when not a lot of people have walked through the area since the prey did.

The Mythbusters television show actually did an episode to see if they could fool scent-detecting dogs with the most commonly thought of deterrents. In a huge warehouse, they hid contraband in peanut butter, coffee, citronella, perfume, and bleach. The dog found it every time. They did another show where they tried to evade a tracking bloodhound with the urban legends of crossing a river, putting pepper on the trail, using a no-scent suit, or hunter's no-scent spray, and none of these worked.

To lose a dog you'd have to hope for a torrential downpour or, at the other end of the spectrum, dry, sunny, hot, desert weather, and terrain that a dog can't handle (like a rock face). Either that or you'd have to find some way to get the dog or tracker to lose interest, or be distracted by something else. Maybe you could get the dog's favourite food, or get some urine of a female dog in heat, but who has those when they are on the run? And even if the dog is distracted momentarily, any good handler will get their canine back on your trail pretty fast.

Dogs are not used just to track people. Pointers and hounds, among others, are also often part of hunting groups to help with tracking animals.

Chapter 17:
Tracking animals

There are lots of reasons people track animals, from hunting to conservation, and photography to ranching. Tracking animals can be pretty fun: they do a lot of neat stuff. You can track animals in the bush or you can track them in urban areas (to find where your dog ran off to or to figure out what walked across your freshly washed truck with muddy paws). Usually you track the species and not a specific animal, but I have been asked to track a wounded animal that a hunter has injured.

The biggest differences in tracking animals instead of people are: animals' senses are way more attuned; they leave different sign; and their routines and behaviour are much more predictable.

More attuned senses

Most animals will hear you coming before you even think about going in their direction. That's why tracking animals when you're on a horse gives you the advantage. Aside from providing safety (most bears won't bother a horse, for instance) and the ability to get away quickly, you're more able to sneak up on your quarry. The four-beat hoof falls of the horse don't spook your quarry and, even as a lump on the horse's back, you don't appear to be a threat to them. I rode through a gang of elks one night and they didn't flinch.

Animals' sense of smell is also typically superior, so you have to think more about your position and want to stay downwind of them. You can try to minimize your smell, but there is no proven method to mask or eliminate it. There's one time you don't have to worry about if you stink or not. If you're tracking a big buck in rut, bucks will literally stick their nose up a doe's butt and become oblivious to the rest of the world (not unlike men in a bar with pretty girls around). Hunters could be fifty yards away from them, and they'd have no clue.

Usually, animals also have better eyesight. That's why camouflage is so important for serious hunters or photographers. I covered camouflage and concealment under evasion tactics pretty thoroughly, so I won't go over it again here, except to say that the hiding techniques differ. Hunters hide behind blinds or stands. Anyone tracking animals has to be prepared to stay very still and quiet for long periods of time. Suffice it to say that sneaking up on wildlife is much more difficult than sneaking up on humans. Maybe that's why we get such a thrill when we see wildlife, and even their sign.

Different sign

On one walk through Pancake Bay Provincial Park's hiking trails (on Lake Superior), you can often see several indicators that moose have been on those same trails. First, you might find a pile of scat; later on, you might spot some tracks in the muddy sections; next, you might notice a couple bare patches on a tree. Then, later, you put one, two, and three together and realize that the bare spots are a moose rub or chew.

Different sign: moose scat; moose tracks in mud; Audrey pointing at a moose rub

That one walk gives you a sense of the different types of ground and top sign you'll see with animals; but let's look at them in more detail.

Potty talk

Leaving scat right on trails is typically not a human trait, so any animal tracker needs to know what its quarry's scat looks like. Any decent animal tracking book has lots of pictures of scat, in addition to the usual info on routines and tracks. I don't spend a lot of time with scat, but I know enough to recognize whose it may be. You should know that bear scat is really dark, with a purple hue during blueberry season. Canines and felines squeeze out small versions of what human turds look like. Coyotes and wolves have whitish scat with hair and bone in it, and their scat often spirals. Deer, moose (most ungulates, I suppose), and bunnies excrete roundish pellets of scat (obviously ranging greatly in size). Ever seen a cow patty? Once it dries out, it could be a disgusting Frisbee. Birds usually have the tell-tale white mixed with brown or black splat as you've seen on plenty a windshield, but Canada geese excrete out thin cylindrical scat that is greenish black and white at the end.

Bear scat, coyote or wolf scat (note the spiral) and goose scat.

Most scat that is bright and shiny is reasonably fresh. If it is steaming, it's even fresher. As it dries, it becomes duller in colour (see the photos on page 48, "Aging: Time of travel"). For aging scat and if you're still wondering what might have made the pile, you could poke it open with a stick to see if there is vegetable matter, bones, or fur, to help you sort out the mystery in the end (pun intended) and the more dry and crumbly or hard that it is the older it is. Be careful handling scat because there are some wicked parasites that can be picked up by handling it with your bare hands.

After poking apart the coyote/ wolf scat with a stick you can see fur and bone pieces confirming your prey is carnivorous.

Here the scat has been washed away, but fur and bone pieces remain

Poking about in poop is putrid and perhaps it isn't even poop, but a pellet (pardon the unplanned alliteration). Owl pellets can be mistaken for scat. They are the regurgitation of all the indigestible bits of bone and fur from the rodents and birds they eat.

Potty talk also wouldn't be complete without some urine talk. Canines like to mark their territory widely by peeing a bit on trees and rocks around their area. Deer do it, too. Also, most wild animals, when they get up in the morning, go to the bathroom. Where they go can even give you clues as to their sex. A doe squats like a human and there will be a urine mark behind where she lay down. A bull or a buck stands up and pees right on top of their bed (I know ladies, I can hear you now: yes, men are pigs).

Later in the day, male deer will scratch the ground bare and pee there. They put their hind legs together, and urinate over the scent glands they have there (when they are in rut) to say to the ladies: "Get a whiff of me...like what you smell? Hang around, I'll be back."

Rubs and scratches

Moving up the line, rubs and scratches are top sign you'll want to look out for. Deer will have a whole trail of rubs and scrapes; they rub the bark off the trees and bushes with their antlers, and there will also be scrapes on the ground where they've just urinated on their scent gland. There will also be an overhanging limb there five to six feet off the ground, where they also rub their scent gland in the outer corner of their eye up against, as a scent post to any doe. They're hoping the doe will like what they smell and wait for them to return. If you want a photo of a deer and you see lots of scrapes and rubs, it's a good place to set up a tree stand.

Elk also use the bush to rub the velvet off their new rack when it gets itchy. You can sometimes even see the velvet on the ground. The colour of their antler tines apparently depends in part on what tree they rubbed against, like if they rub on a poplar tree, the rack is much darker.

One time I thought that the poplar tree I was looking at had an elk rub on it, but my pal told me that it was from a moose chewing on it. Looking closer at the branch, the teeth marks were unmistakeable.

Here's a branch chewed by an animal in Northern Ontario. It's probably not a moose considering how precise it is, it's more likely from a porcupine, a rabbit or hare (during winter).

Bears and cats (cougars, bobcats, etc.) also leave marks on trees, but they leave scratches. Ever heard of or seen a bear tree? Bears like to play king of the castle and see how they measure up to others in the area. Since there is no locker room that they all change in, the bear stands up and scratches as high as it can up the tree. It's a clear signal to other bears that if their scratches aren't the top ones, there is a bigger bear in town...and these woods might not be big enough for the two of them. There used to be one big bear tree west of Turner Valley with hundreds of bear scratches on it.

Other sign

Vegetation eaten by animals (deer, rabbits, cats) or gnawed trees (beavers), and vegetation disturbances like broken-off branches or bent grasses or tall plants are all other top sign. Years ago, I read somewhere that rabbits chew off branches sharply at a 45-degree angle and I wouldn't have believed it until I saw it.

The rabbit on the left chewed the vegetation on the right – note the 45 degree angle

Deer aren't so tidy, they just rip at twigs and branches. Moose like to eat willows and vegetation smaller in diameter than a finger. They'll level off a whole area like a tall weed-whacker and then move on. They also love water lilies in the spring when they're the most tender, so, once again, sometimes the absence of sign is sign.

Beaver chewed branch. Moose browse (at shoulder height), notice the white chewed ends on this bush.

Of course, animals walking through an area disturb a lot less than humans would, but animals damage a lot more from nibbling at everything (unlike humans). Animals with hooves tend to lift their feet almost straight up and then put them straight down. Not only does that make them quieter and leave smaller tracks, but the vegetation barely gets moved and the ground doesn't get pushed or dragged forward.

Fur is ground sign, but it's top sign if it is snagged in a tree. Reptiles will shed their skin and leave that behind, too; but like I said before, you'll NEVER catch me tracking snakes. Another type of shed that is more interesting is antlers (also known as **sheds**), which can be sold to collectors, especially if both sheds are found. (Though I have heard that they now sell owl pellet dissection kits, so maybe collecting pellets will become all the rage.)

Fur is ground sign

Antlers (sheds) are quite collectable

Other animal ground sign includes trails, runs, dens, burrows, and beds. Animals, like humans, will use the same trails and stay on them for easy walking. Frequently- and infrequently-used animal trails and runs to and from feeding areas, watering holes, dens, etc., are a great place to stake out if you're looking for animals and want to see their tracks, or see what certain movement looks like in tracks. When I didn't understand animal tracks I was seeing, I'd look for a place like this and wait to see a deer turn and jump, and then go look at the tracks to see what that looked like. The more I did that, the more I learned.

Animal trail through tall brush. Animal trail through tall grass. Animal trails left in a panne at Sandbanks Provincial Park, in Ontario.

Squirrels that dig up or bury food caches, or animals (like cats) that cover scat also leave ground sign in the form of scratches.

Animals' scent can also be a bit of a giveaway, especially if you're following a bear that loves to roll around in dead animal carcasses: so it's not top or ground sign, but it's still sign. Lastly, as already discussed, deer act different around bears or a pack of wolves, so you can always see what other animals in the area are doing to potentially signal to you where your quarry might be. And when you're up tracking other animals, always beware of animals that might be tracking you.

Profiling

The psychology of tracking still applies to animals, but there is less in-species variation. If you want to be a good cowboy, you've got to think like a cow and put yourself in its hooves.

The same goes for any wildlife you're tracking, you have to know their routines.

You start by understanding the relatively predictable patterns of the species, and what their tracks and scat look like. Then you can research local variations in routine, like favourite watering holes and known runs. Some animals are so patterned in their behaviour, that if you wanted to see an elk at certain ranches, you just went to 'X' spot to see them at 2pm. Animals' patterns aren't complicated. They hunt, eat, drink, sleep, mate, and excrete. So they're either going to or from the feed ground, bed ground, mating ground, or water. Humans should be so easy to track, but they're not, they can be all over like a duck's butt (you ever watch a duck walk?). So back to animals, here's some of what I've noticed in profiling animals.

- *Cows are easy to track. They stick to trails, unless they get spooked; they prefer taking the route of least resistance, just like people in a hurry. Also, watching a group of cows, you get to know which cows are going to bolt. If a cow is a little high-headed, she's looking for a hole. Some people might not see it at first, but you start to notice subtle cues and differences, and the cow that is doing things just a bit differently is the one to watch. In those times, a good cowboy learns to move his horse ten feet ahead of the cow to cut off the animal's path proactively. The rookie cowboy reacts to what happens; and he's typically a bit too late.*
- *Deer bed down during the day, graze at last light, and take naps. Whitetails are more prevalent near grain fields, and mule deer are typically higher up.*
- *Bears are very opportunistic. While they're happy to eat grass, if they smell a dead animal, they'll be the first to chew on that, bury the leftovers for a few days, go back and uncover it, and maybe even roll around in it.*
- *Grouse might fly up eight feet into a tree, but other than that, they pretty much stay close to the ground. (John Siebert, an old cowboy I worked with at the Turner Valley Ranch, said: "We should fly – everything else with two feet does." Well John, everything except penguins, ostriches, emus, and kiwis – or so I've since been told).*

- *Wounded animals gravitate downhill. On the second day, they start to get a fever and stay by water. They won't go very far if they find decent shelter and water.*
- *Wounded elk will get away from the herd, to keep the herd safe since they're the weakest link. (I once tracked a wounded elk for half a mile for a hunter, and I expected to find it dead. I jumped over a fence and there was a six-point bull elk, looking like he was going to make a stand; luckily, he didn't charge.)*
- *Bears, when wounded, will go through piles of brush and knock over trees to find a place to hide and lick their wounds or expire. If you suspect the amount of sign (including blood) might belong to a wounded animal, beware: they can be mighty cranky when they're hurt.*

Wounded animals and animals in rut are truly unpredictable, so you have to take particular caution. Animals can also surprise you with how smart they are. While I said animals don't have a lot of evasive manoeuvres, that may be a bit misleading, because they do all kinds of things to avoid detection by their predators. The difference is that there are fewer techniques and they are easier to learn. Hiding, camouflage, and quiet movement are their most common evasive manoeuvres.

My Uncle Jerry was out hunting once when he saw bear tracks and decided to follow them. It didn't take him long to realize that where the bear had gone had been vantage points for the bear to watch him. The bear had turned the tables on Uncle Jerry and was tracking him. It spooked Uncle Jerry a little and we all learned that bears are smarter than you think. Not unlike my Uncle Jerry, I'm not really a fan of those big brown buggers. Bluff charging is another of their evasive or defensive manoeuvres. A bear, especially a young bear, will run straight at you (or your horse), then suddenly stop ten feet away, hoping to make you run.

Overall, you need to know when, where, and what your quarry eats and hunts, and what its scat and other common sign are. Then go to where you're most likely to find a track. When you find one, you determine the direction and speed of travel, and, given your location, determine if you think the animal is on its way to hunt or returning home, or going for a drink, etc. The first thing that you want to identify, though, is if it is the right species! Knowing basic tracks will help.

Identifying animal tracks

When looking at an animal track, start by looking at the size of the track and the number of toes to determine the family of animal and the species.

Looking at these bird tracks compared to the human tracks makes it obvious that these are big birds: Canada goose across the bottom of the photo and Great Blue Heron walking towards the top of the photo. Great Blue Heron

Canines and felines

Animals in the cat and dog families have four toes. Size is one way to discern which is which. To tell whether the animal is from the cat or the dog family, look at the pattern of the tracks and the claw marks. Felines place their back feet in line with their front paws. This is known as direct register. Canines place their feet close to, but not directly in, the same track. This is called an indirect register.

The other distinguishing feature is claw marks. The cat family retract their claws when they walk, so there are no claw marks in their tracks. The dog family, including wolves and coyotes, leave their claws out. Interestingly enough, only the two middle claws show in coyote tracks, but dogs, wolves, and foxes' tracks show all four claws.

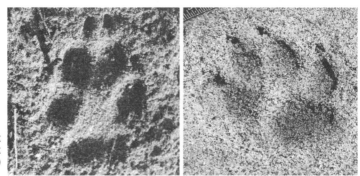

Coyote track
(left), dog track
(right)

Ungulates

Hoofed mammals like deer, moose, and cows, make an upside-down heart-shaped track made up of two teardrop shapes stuck together. Unlike other animal families, their tracks change significantly with speed of travel. As mentioned in "Direction and speed of travel" when whitetail deer and moose are running, the two teardrops split apart.

The moose is not running in the first photo, but it is in the second. Not only are the teardrop toes apart in the second photo, but also look at the toe kick from a speedy pace.

Littler fur balls (and one big one)

Rodents, including mice, chipmunks, squirrels, porcupines, and beavers (yes, Canada's national animal is a rodent), have four toes up front and five on their hind feet. The size of the tracks will obviously help you determine a mouse from a beaver; if there is a thin line showing a tail drag, it isn't from a chipmunk or squirrel.

Rabbits' toes are very close together and don't show up well in tracks. Their tracks are actually most distinguishable by the pair of small tracks at the back and the large tracks at the front. The larger tracks are made by the rear feet, which launch ahead of the front feet as the rabbit or hare is hopping quickly.

Bears, raccoons, and skunks all have five toes and their claw marks are often visible in the track. Bears have a large pad with close-set toes and claws (the photo of a bear track as top sign was on page 15 under "Tracking and sign awareness"); raccoons have long toes and their tracks look like a really small child's hand print.

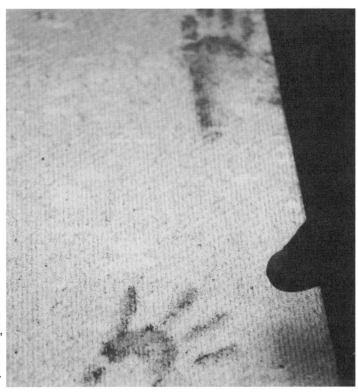

And here's the answer to the photo under "Urban Tracking" (page 112): these are raccoon tracks.

Anyone who spends enough time in the bush will have at least a couple of close-call bear stories, even if they only saw the bear tracks (like with my Uncle Jerry). Many a time when I was leaving a valley, there were fresh bear tracks on top of my horse's tracks. There was bush on both sides, and the bear could've easily been ten yards from me and I wouldn't have seen him. One of those bear tracks had a seven-inch pad.

If for no other reason than to tell your friends a good campfire story, to find out how long the bear is you measure the width of the bear pad (in inches) and add one to it. That number is the number of feet long that the bear is, nose to tail. So, a seven-inch pad means that there was an eight-foot bear really close by. To estimate how tall the bear would have been standing, add another one or one and a half to the paw pad plus one measure. In the case of the example, the bear would have been nine to ten feet tall, standing. It's a little too late to get scared at that point. You have to pay attention, keep your wits about you, and hopefully get to where you're going.

Chapter 18:
A final word, or two

"Take only photographs, leave only footprints."

Unknown

"We abuse the land because we regard it as a commodity belonging to us. When we see land as a community to which we belong, we may begin to use it with love and respect."

Aldo Leopold

"We're in front of electronics too much. If you have to focus on a screen, make it the screen door...on your way out."

Nadine Robinson

So there you have it, 40 years of experience in tracking two- and four-legged beasts wrapped up like a calf at stampede. Sure, we could have added more examples, but sometimes less is more.

Getting these last words down, it's hard not to think back to the beginning of this journey, when I was approached with the idea of writing a book. I really wasn't sure what we'd write or how we'd do it. Along the way, it became clear that writing and tracking weren't so different. They're both usually solitary journeys, but can be even more fun when shared with the right person. Both require keen powers of observation. Both take dogged determination and perseverance. Tracking and writing are also both crafts that have to be honed with practice, and there aren't any shortcuts to make either happen.

A track is truly like one word in a sentence. That word can be taken out of context if the other words alongside it aren't read properly. After reading one word, you move on to the next, see how they string together, and see if they make sense. Pushing the analogy, as sentences come together to form paragraphs and chapters that tell a story, so various strings of sign come together to tell the story of a prey's journey. Maybe the only difference between writing and tracking is that, in tracking, you don't usually start reading at the first word on the first page, you're stepping into a sentence in progress, and sometimes have to go backwards before you can go forwards to understand the whole story.

Lucky for me, while I know tracking, Nadine knows writing. She was the right "sidekick" for this project, even though she knew nothing about tracking going in. As she said to me at our first meeting, "Terry, if you can make *me* understand tracking, *I* can make everyone else understand it too." Having been out in the bush with me in Alberta and in Northern Ontario for hours on end, and after listening to me spin more yarn than a sweater factory has in inventory, she's now a tracker in her own right, and I think that she's done a fine job getting the ideas across to you.

We hope that this book has taught you the basics of tracking, or refreshed your existing skills. We want to give you new eyes, like a child looking around at the world for the first time. With any luck, after reading this book, you're already looking at the world differently, focusing on new things.

Our ultimate goal is for you to be able to follow tracks until you find your prey still standing in them, or at least make you more track aware and interested in getting outdoors. No matter how far you've strayed from nature, you can always come back to it and be renewed by it.

The news is full of stories about kids spending as much time in front of screens as their parents spend at work. There's nothing right about that. We're putting too much value on televisions, laptops, tablets, smart phones, and the stuff coming out of them. The screen we'd like to see used a lot more is the screen door, so that people get up off the couch and get outside.

Get out and test your new-found skills. Breathe in the fresh air, appreciate the wilderness, and don't forget to pack out everything that you packed in. If you're close to nature, you can't ignore what's happening to it. Nature doesn't lie, cheat, or steal. It isn't greedy. It's always there and doesn't expect anything from you, but you have a responsibility to look after it: respect it.

You're probably gathering that this is more than a tracking book, and it is. Tracking is a way of life that encourages caring about the world and to the people around you – and paying attention to them. It's about living fully, being present, and not letting the should'ves, could'ves, would'ves, mustn'ts, and didn'ts hold you back. The back trail of the tracks of your life is already written, but your next steps aren't. Whether you move straight ahead, or double back, or make a 90-degree turn, you're in control of your future direction.

If you can see more tracking in your future, check out the references section that follows, come on out and take a course with me, and think about volunteering for Search and Rescue in your area. Not ready to volunteer? SAR organizations across the continent are not-for-profits and can always use your donation.

With that said, if this book were me out ranching, I'd be on my ride home about now, ready to have a bean and tip my hat over my eyes for the night.

I'm passing you the reins. Now it's up to you to keep the art of tracking alive.

Happy tracking. Happy trails!

About the authors

Terry Grant was the face of the hit television show Mantracker for six seasons. Raised in Ontario, Terry headed west as soon as he got his driver's licence and worked as a cowboy for legendary Alberta ranches like the Bar-U and the OH for close to 25 years. While in Alberta, he honed his animal tracking skills as a cowboy, hunter, guide, and outfitter. Terry is a seasoned Search and Rescue professional, having worked with the Foothills, Alberta Search and Rescue Team for more than 12 years. His reputation as a tracker impressed the British military, which enlisted his expertise to help soldiers identify hidden improvised explosive devices (IEDs). Calgary made him a "white hatter" in 2011, and Terry continues to volunteer at the Calgary Stampede annually. He lives near High River, Alberta and when he's not on the back of his horse, Terry can be found in his shop working on his custom carpentry, out on the golf course, or playing with his border collies. In addition to this book, Terry offers courses for those interested in the art of tracking. See www.trackingwithterry.com.

Nadine Robinson is a freelance writer and newspaper columnist from Ontario. Raised in Ottawa, she has travelled the world, speaks several languages, and has worked in Mexico, Argentina, and Canada. Nadine holds a Bachelor of Commerce from Carleton University, an International MBA from the University of Ottawa, and is currently completing her Doctorate in Business Administration at Athabasca University. She's a part-time professor at Algoma University in Sault Ste. Marie, where she's raising her daughter Audrey and son Andrew. Nadine believes that life is for living, and she enjoys attempting things that make her a little uncomfortable; like learning to ride a dirt bike, or co-authoring this, her first book.

How they met

Lawrence Foster, the chase supervisor and prey cameraman on the Mantracker series, is a friend of Nadine's. One day, she asked Lawrence: "When the heck is Terry Grant going to write a book?" When Terry was in "the Sault" in 2009, Lawrence set up a lunch meeting, and Nadine got to ask Terry himself...and so it began.

Acknowledgements

From Terry

To all the people I've met in SAR over the years, and to all the people and situations in life that made me a better tracker, I thank you. To Dewy for tilting his hat my way for the Mantracker series, to all of the prey who made the chase so much fun, and to Bonterra Productions & OLN, thanks for the great ride...it was awesome.

I'd also like to express my gratitude to my friends including Roger Bellerose and Guy Kerr, who proofread sections of the book, and gave us suggestions that made our book better. The cover also wouldn't look as cool without the design skills of Tiina Keranen, not to mention the footprint logo designed for me by Darby Davey.

A big thank you goes out to Lawrence for taking me to lunch that day in 2009, to meet one smart cookie with a heck of a way with words. Nadine heard me say, "Work, work, work, I love it. I could watch it all day," but seriously... to Nadine, a sincere thank you for all your hard work, this wouldn't have happened without you.

And a final thank you to FriesenPress (Lisa and Jordan in particular). Thanks to them, we're able to donate part of the proceeds and still have something left over for us.

From Nadine

To the Ottawa Citizen for publishing my first article over a decade ago, and to the Sault Star for giving me a column for the past four years; thank you for allowing me to call myself a writer. To all of my "columny," family, friends, and students, I'm grateful for your encouragement.

To my mom, Penny Sipkes, to my sister, Denise Robinson, to Diane Ryerson, Brian Houle, and Karen Pomber, thank you for editing me to clarity on this and other projects. Paul, Michael, and Rick, thank you for believing in this book.

To Jerry and June Demers (of Agawa Indian Crafts) I can't thank you enough for providing me with the solitude required to complete this project.

To the Foster boys, this book wouldn't exist without the introduction from one of you and the loving support of the other. Steve, words don't capture how much I thank you for believing in me and my dreams. I'm also grateful that you were willing to interrupt our fun for me take photos, and to take some for me too. Thank you to my children, Audrey and Andrew, for allowing me to get away with writing "just one more sentence" on more than one occasion.

And last, but not least, thank you to Terry for letting me bring his years of experience to the world through this book...I am truly honoured, and I only hope that my next project (whatever it will be) is as much fun.

Glossary & Index

Excrement human feces, *15*

Evasion/evasive techniques anti-tracking techniques used when the prey does not want to be seen or found, *4, 141, 143, 155-163, 182*

Feces waste expelled from an animal, aka poop, doo doo, crap, excrement, scat, etc., *7, 14, 15*

FLIR forward-looking infrared, *165*

Gait speed of travel, *41, 45, 64*

GPS Global Positioning System, *8, 66, 67, 151, 152, 166*

Ground sign sign found on the ground, *14, 15, 17, 20, 26, 36, 50, 73, 86, 120, 122, 189, 190*

Hasty Team a three-person tracking team in SAR made up of a tracker, a navigator, and a person in charge of communications and first-aid, *70, 130, 131-136, 144, 164*

Heel strike the first imprint made by your heel when you take a step, *41, 42, 43, 44, 82, 101*

Jump tracking a tracking technique used to move quickly/gain ground on prey by assuming a continued direction of travel along a path, road, or open field involving jumping ahead to find corroborating sign. Even if the prey veers off the path and comes back, the tracker does not divert their course to investigate, *113, 114, 115-116, 117, 124, 136*

LKP SAR acronym for **last known position** or **last known point** (interchangeable with PLK). Usually for air searches, like the coordinates called in with a mayday, *128, 129, 131, 135, 140, 143, 160*

Lope slow gallop, *24, 169, 175*

Lost soul or **misper** (missing person) Search and Rescue term for a person who has gone missing outside of urban settings. They're also referred to as "the missing" or "the lost", *2, 29, 105, 115, 116, 120, 124-144, 145, 165, 167, 178*

Negative imprint an indentation left where a rock or stick used to be that has since been kicked, moved, stepped on and pushed, or tripped over, *38, 53, 80, 82, 86*

Northumberland rain dance a method of determining the critical search spacing in SAR based on terrain, topography, weather, time of day and the object sought. It was developed by two mathematicians involved in SAR in Northumberland, UK, *137-139*

Pitch the relative distance off centre that a track is angled, *40, 41, 102*

PLK SAR acronym for the **place last known** (see LKP)

PLS SAR acronym for the **place last seen**, *126, 128, 129, 135, 140, 143*

POA SAR acronym for **probability of area**, which is the likelihood that what they're searching for will be in that area, *128, 129*

POD SAR acronym for **probability of detection**, or the likelihood that they'll find what the search object if it is in the search area, *128, 129, 139*

POS SAR acronym for **probability of success**, or the likelihood of finding what they're searching for given the POA and POD, *129*

Prey what is being tracked. Also called quarry, game, the hunted, the missing, lost souls (in Search and Rescue), *2*

Quad all-terrain vehicle (also known as an ATV), *129, 177*

ROW SAR acronym for **rest of world**, aka the area outside the AOD, *128*

Rut the mating season for mammals; male animals in rut get careless when females are about and aggressive when other males are in their area; comes from the Latin word for roar, *33, 171, 182, 186, 192*

Runs trails used over and over by rabbits, *119, 190, 191*

SAR acronym for Search and Rescue, *28, 60, 66, 70, 105, 114, 125-147, 199, 210*

Scat animal feces, *7, 15, 48, 83, 182-186, 190*

Sheds shed antlers (quite valuable to collectors especially if both sheds are found), *189*

Shine, the silvery imprint from walking in moccasins or light-tread running shoes down a dirt road; is not apparent up close but can be seen at an angle from a distance, *18-19, 23, 24, 37, 85, 101, 115, 169*

Sign anything left, moved, taken, or changed by a person or animal as they pass through an area. Also called "spoor," sign is everything that can point you towards your prey, *3, 14-16, 37, 73-113, 157,182-189*

Sign-aware/sign awareness knowing where to look for sign, and what to look for while tracking, *14-16, 115*

Sign-cutting a SAR term for tracking/finding sign, *14*

Skidder trails old logging paths, *66*

Sky-lined/sky-lining when prey put themselves between you and the sky – like they are walking along the crest of a hill or a ridge. **Sky-lining** is good for trackers and bad for prey because it's always easier to see movement against a backdrop of sky than against the forest floor, *26, 157*

Spoor a Dutch word meaning track, adopted by hunters in Africa, *14*

Step a SAR term for the distance between the heel of one track and the heel of the next track – which is marked on the tracking stick, *20, 38, 40-41, 45, 101, 102, 111, 132*

Step-by-step tracking a method of tracking where you find each track before moving on to the next track (used in SAR), *114-117, 131, 136, 144, 155*

Straddle the distance between the inside of the right and left tracks, *40-41*

Stride SAR term for the length of two steps: the distance between the heel of your right foot to the heel of your right foot when it strikes the ground again. For measuring distances in SAR when you don't have a GPS, *20, 40-41, 45, 101, 102, 111, 132*

Toe kick the dirt plume spreading out from behind a track; left from a person's toes pushing off the ground to move forwards, *19, 41-45, 86, 92, 93, 102, 105, 106, 107, 194*

Topo short for topographic

Topographic or topographical map a map of an area that has contour lines that show elevation, depression of landscape, and marks features of an area: water, vegetation, roads, highways, etc., *65-66, 67, 128, 166*

Top sign sign found above the ground, typically at knee or shoulder level, *15, 17, 29, 73, 86, 122, 126, 135, 183, 186, 187, 189, 195*

Track a footprint, paw print, or hoof print; it is an example of ground sign, *14, 17-24, 36-55, 85-111, 132-134, 193-196*

Track trap a natural or man-made area where if someone passes through it, they are bound to leave sign, *94, 117-118*

Track width measurement across the ball of the foot of the track, *20, 132*

Track length measurement from the tip of the toe to the end of the heel, *21, 132*

Tracking the art of identifying and interpreting sign to find your prey, or determine relevant information about them, *2, 5-8, 14,*
...

Tracking stick any kind of stick or pole that is not cumbersome to carry, like an old ski pole, hiking stick, cane, or stick you find in the forest that you mark the width and length of the track on, and also the step, to help you find more sign, *20-22, 38, 45, 69, 115, 132, 134*

Trail a series of tracks or sign from one person or a group of people; a nice place to take a walk in the woods that is often groomed for that purpose; a path used repeatedly by animals (game trail), *16, 23, 24, 38, 46, 58, 60, 73, 88, 115, 135, 169, 178, 190*

Ungulate a mammal with hooves, *45, 80, 184, 189, 194*

Metric conversion

I'm not too consistent in the way I use distances and weights. You've probably noticed me refer to miles, inches, feet, yards, and I'm not sure what else. In Canada, the metric system wasn't introduced until after I'd finished with school (or it had finished with me), so here are some conversions for you if you're wondering.

1 mile	=	1,760 yd	=	1.609 km
1 yard	=	3 feet	=	0.914 m
1 foot	=	12 inches	=	30.48 cm
1 inch	=	2.54 cm		

1 km	=	0.621 miles
1 meter	=	1.093 yards

1 pound (lb)	=	.4536 kg
1 kg	=	2.204 lbs

References

Search and Rescue

National Search and Rescue Secretariat (NSS)
www.nss.gc.ca

Search and Rescue Volunteer Association of Canada (SARVAC)
www.sarvac.ca

Foothills Search and Rescue Society
www.foothills-sar.ca

Emergency Response Institute
www.ericanada.com

Civil Air Search and Rescue Association
www.CASARA.ca

U.S. SAR Task Force
www.ussartf.org

Search dogs

The Canadian Search Dog Association
www.canadiansearchdog.com

Search and Rescue Dogs of the United States (SARDUS)
www.sardogsus.org

Child survival sites and educational programs

ChildFind
www.childfind.ca

Hug-a-Tree and Survive
www.rcmp-grc.gc.ca/hugtree-presarbre/prog-eng.htm

E-mail: hugatree@rcmp-grc.gc.ca

Hug-a-Tree and Survive Canada
c/o Search and Rescue Section
RCMP National HQ
1200 Vanier Parkway,
Ottawa, ON K1A 0R2

Lost in the Woods - Child Survival for Parents and Teachers (book by Colleen Politano)

www.ussartf.org/child_survival_.htm
www.foothills-sar.ca/lost-in-the-woods/

Other important references

Terry Grant's website
www.trackingwithterry.com

Nadine Robinson's website
www.theink.ca

Mantracking Facebook page
http://www.facebook.com/Mantracking

Like us on Facebook!

Feedback

We want to hear what you think, and if you post photos or examples you might end up in the next book! Post your feedback on the Mantracking Facebook page: http://www.facebook.com/Mantracking

Sign up for Terry's newsletter on his website to get all the latest news.

To book Terry for speaking engagements and/or to learn more about his tracking courses, go to www.trackingwithterry.com

Requests to book Nadine for speaking engagements go to nadine@mantracking.ca

Fundraising & Corporate orders

Want to sell this book as a fundraiser for your organization? We can help – email us at fundraising@mantracking.ca. If you would like a volume discount to use books for educational purposes, or to gift the books to employees or clients, contact sales@mantracking.ca.

The end

Notes

Notes